"We pray the church's liturgical prayers at night—Compline—because they give us words when we don't know what to say, and they give us better words to say than we might give. This little book is holy glow in your hands: read it, savor it, and most of all join Tish Harrison Warren in prayer in the quiet of the night. Those who pray well are honest, vulnerable, frustrated, hopeful, learning, and most of all they are listeners—all on display in *Prayer in the Night*. But don't let the beauty of this book captivate you; let its subject capture you into becoming a person of prayer."

Scot McKnight, professor of New Testament at Northern Seminary

"In the tradition of Anglican poet-theologian memoirists like Elisabeth Elliot and Barbara Brown Taylor, Tish Harrison Warren offers a personal exploration of the evergreen problem of theodicy. And like the prayer from the Book of Common Prayer that it unfolds, this lovely book holds out the light of Christ to us at a time when the shadows in our world seem only to grow longer."

Wesley Hill, associate professor of New Testament at Trinity School for Ministry in Ambridge, Pennsylvania, and author of *Spiritual Friendship*

"The prayers of the saints have brought me great comfort over the years, not only giving me language to express my deepest fears and best hopes to God but also reminding me that I'm not alone. Tish Harrison Warren has walked through dark valleys, has clung to Jesus by clinging to these prayers, and now offers up a treasure of hard-won wisdom. Reading this book was like sitting with a friend who keeps watch in the night, reminding me of the patient presence of God."

Andrew Peterson, singer/songwriter and author of *Adorning the Dark*

"*Prayer in the Night* is another radiant example of wisdom formed in the crucible of suffering. As a priest who finds she can't pray, Tish Harrison Warren finds God in our harrowing vulnerability—and stubbornly holds to believing that God remains good even when life is not. This is a book I'll turn to again and again when life is upended. It's a book I will put into the hands of suffering friends. *Prayer in the Night* is a book that sings, even as it weeps."

Jen Pollock Michel, author of *Surprised by Paradox*

"Tish has done it again! Good writers, Frederick Buechner once told me, 'pay attention to their lives.' By this standard, Tish Harrison Warren is a very good writer indeed. She tells stories from her own life—sometimes commonplace, sometimes heartbreaking—with great detail, and even greater insight. Using the brilliant, time-tested words found in Compline, a service of evening prayers used before sleep, as her outline, this well-written and deeply honest book will inspire you to begin using these prayers in your own life. It did for me. Reading this book was like having a meaningful conversation with a friend over a crackling fire and having a clear sense that you are the better for having engaged in it. Tish is far too young to be this wise. I am grateful for her life, for her searching faith, and I am very grateful for this special book."

James Bryan Smith, author of *The Good and Beautiful God*

"I know of few writers today who write as pastorally, prophetically, and poetically as Tish Harrison Warren. I know of few writers of any time who write of the deep, dark stuff of life with as much hope, grace, and beauty as you will find in these pages. *Prayer in the Night* will bring to the darkness in your life a light that will carry you through the days."

Karen Swallow Prior, author of *On Reading Well* and *Fierce Convictions*

"To be creatures is to face many nights: the darkness of the unknown, the un-certain, the unseen. God, in his grace, does not promise to expel the dark; he promises to be with us in the night. In prose that is both powerful and vulnerable, Tish Harrison Warren invites us to receive Compline as a gift to help us face the dark. Prayer is how we press our hands into the invisible and find the hand of Christ reaching back."

James K. A. Smith, Calvin University, author of *You Are What You Love*

"By the light of an ancient nighttime prayer, this book tenderly and thoroughly explores the beautiful and precarious reality of our shared human life. And it illuminates for us the ultimate Christian question: what it means to love and be loved by a God who made us as vulnerable as we are, and also made himself as vulnerable as we are."

Andy Crouch, author of *Culture Making* and *Strong and Weak*

"In *Prayer in the Night*, Tish Harrison Warren once again ingeniously mines the beauty and wonder of the ordinary, especially in what some might take for granted or neglect: night prayer—Compline for those familiar with the Divine Office. She considers well the implications of God's presence, not only in the midst of our nights, wherever and however we find ourselves, but also amid the dark nights of our souls. Through Compline, we are drawn to pray for and re-member others in their nights. As Tish notes, 'Christian discipleship is a lifetime of training in how to pay attention to the right things, to notice God's work in our lives and in the world.' And that is exactly what Tish so expertly does and beckons us to do through this book. It is a beautiful offering."

Marlena Graves, author of *The Way Up Is Down: Becoming Yourself by Forgetting Yourself*

"This book is the rare combination of beautiful prose and weighty theological reflection. It paints a picture of a faith that is still there on the other side of trite, easy answers that do not satisfy, a picture of hard-won belief. This is not just a book about prayer; at times the book becomes a prayer in its own right. It is, in the end, a reflection on what it means to be a Christian in the midst of losses large and small. I highly recommend it."

Esau McCaulley, author of *Reading While Black*

Prayer
in the
Night

*For Those Who Work
or Watch or Weep*

Tish Harrison Warren

An imprint of InterVarsity Press
Downers Grove, Illinois

InterVarsity Press
P.O. Box 1400, Downers Grove, IL 60515-1426
ivpress.com
email@ivpress.com

InterVarsity Press® is the book-publishing division of InterVarsity Christian Fellowship/USA®, a movement of students and faculty active on campus at hundreds of universities, colleges, and schools of nursing in the United States of America, and a member movement of the International Fellowship of Evangelical Students. For information about local and regional activities, visit intervarsity.org.

Scripture quotations, unless otherwise noted, are from The Holy Bible, English Standard Version, copyright © 2001 by Crossway Bibles, a division of Good News Publishers. Used by permission. All rights reserved.

While any stories in this book are true, some names and identifying information may have been changed to protect the privacy of individuals.

Cover design and image composite: David Fassett
Interior design: Daniel van Loon
Images: space image: © Level1studio / The Image Bank / Getty Images
    shot of star field: © John Owens / EyeEm / Getty Images
    night sky watercolor: © Khaneeros / iStock / Getty Images Plus

ISBN 978-0-8308-4679-5 (print)
ISBN 978-0-8308-4680-1 (digital)

Printed in the United States of America ♾

InterVarsity Press is committed to ecological stewardship and to the conservation of natural resources in all our operations. This book was printed using sustainably sourced paper.

Library of Congress Cataloging-in-Publication Data
A catalog record for this book is available from the Library of Congress.

P   25 24 23 22 21 20 19 18 17 16 15 14 13 12 11 10 9 8 7 6 5 4 3 2 1
Y   41 40 39 38 37 36 35 34 33 32 31 30 29 28 27 26 25 24 23 22 21

To Raine, Flannery, and Augustine

May God keep watch with you through

every dark night and teach you, day by day,

that it is all for love's sake.

Keep watch, dear Lord, with those who work, or watch,
or weep this night, and give your angels charge over those
who sleep. Tend the sick, Lord Christ; give rest to the
weary, bless the dying, soothe the suffering, pity the afflicted,
shield the joyous; and all for your love's sake. Amen.

BOOK OF COMMON PRAYER

Contents

Author's Note

I AM FINISHING THIS BOOK in early Eastertide 2020 and sending it out to an uncertain world. A pandemic has spread around the globe, death tolls are mounting, and we in the United States have largely been under stay-at-home orders. I have chosen not to specifically address the pandemic in these pages. When I wrote this manuscript, Covid-19 did not exist. By the time this book is released, any reader will likely have far more insight into the reality of Covid-19 and its effects on the world than I could give here. What is needed now is the slow work of wisdom, and I am too near the outset of this tragedy to offer that in any detail.

But though I do not know what lies ahead, I know that whatever awaits us in this particular catastrophe, it will not be the last. We will face other natural disasters and global calamities. And there will be devastating yet more commonplace suffering that each reader will bring to these pages: personal stories of pain, vulnerability, anxiety, and loss that will continue long after the current crisis ends.

So I send this book out with a prayer that it will bear light and truth, and do the work it's been given to do.

Part One

Praying in
the Dark

*Darkness—night—these are always
symbols for the God-forsakenness of the
world . . . and for the lostness of men and
women. In the darkness we see nothing,
and no longer know where we are.*

Jurgen Moltmann, In the End—the Beginning

*Comprehension of good and evil is
given . . . in night fears when we are
small, in dread of the beast's fangs
and in the terror of dark rooms.*

Czeslaw Milosz, One More Day

Prologue

IN THE MIDDLE OF THE NIGHT, covered in blood in an emergency room, I was praying.

We had lived in Pittsburgh for less than a month. Amid frigid nights and snow that had turned to gray slush, I was miscarrying.

Earlier that night, we had joined new acquaintances at their house for dinner. Their daughter went to school with ours. I was two days into the miscarriage, but my doctor had told me to go about the week as planned, so we went. As my husband, Jonathan, made the kind of awkward small talk you rehearse with near strangers, I began to have contractions. I felt like I couldn't quite breathe. I asked to go to an urgent care clinic. I was trying to be breezy and undramatic—not the emergency room, but urgent care, the place where people go for stitches, no big deal.

Jonathan began to explain to our hosts that we had to end the evening early because, though we hadn't mentioned it over dinner pleasantries, I was in the middle of a miscarriage, and while I was supposed to be bleeding slowly for a week, now I was bleeding quickly and in pain. I stood apologizing to our dinner hosts—because as a woman from the South, there is no awkward social situation in which I won't compulsively apologize. Then, suddenly, I began gushing blood. Gushing. I looked like a gunshot victim.

Our hosts threw two towels to my husband, which he wrapped around me as I stumbled into the car, shouting, "Where is the hospital?" We left our children upstairs playing, without saying goodbye, with people whose last name we couldn't quite remember.

It was dark out now. We wound through blurred city lights and hip college students walking to bars. On the way to the hospital I felt faint. Blood quickly soaked both towels as Jonathan offered panicked prayers: "Help her! Breathe. Oh God." He ran all the red lights. He thought I was going to die on the way.

But we made it to the hospital. I was going to be okay, but I needed surgery.

The room filled with nurses, all commenting that this was way more blood than they usually saw, which should have been discomforting, except they seemed calm about it, even a bit fascinated, like I was a particularly well-done project at a school science fair. They put in a line for a blood transfusion, and told me to lie still. Then, I yelled to Jonathan, lost amidst the nurses, "Compline! I want to pray Compline."

It isn't normal—even for me—to loudly demand liturgical prayers in a crowded room in the midst of crisis. But in that moment, I needed it, as much as I needed the IV.

Relieved to have a direct command, Jonathan pulled up the Book of Common Prayer on his phone and warned the nurses, "We are both priests, and we're going to pray now." And then he launched in: "The Lord grant us a peaceful night and a perfect end."

Over the metronome beat of my heart monitor, we prayed the entire nighttime prayer service. I repeated the words by heart as waves of blood flowed from me with each contraction.

"Keep us as the apple of your eye."

"Hide us under the shadow of your wing."

"Lord have mercy. Christ, have mercy. Lord, have mercy."

"Defend us, Lord, from the perils and dangers of this night."

We finished: "The almighty and merciful Lord, Father, Son, and Holy Spirit, bless us and keep us. Amen."

"That's beautiful," one of the nurses said. "I've never heard that before."

✦ ✦ ✦

Why did I suddenly and desperately want to pray Compline underneath the fluorescent lights of a hospital room?

Because I wanted to pray but couldn't drum up words.

It isn't that "Help! Make the bleeding stop!" wasn't holy or sophisticated enough. I was in a paper-thin hospital gown soaked with blood. This was not the time for formality. I wanted healing—but I needed more than just healing. I needed this moment of crisis to find its place in something greater: the prayers of the church, yes, but more, the vast mystery of God, the surety of God's power, the reassurance of God's goodness.

I had to decide again, in that moment, when I didn't know how things would turn out, with my baby dead and my body broken, whether these things I preached about God loving me and being for me were true. Yet I was bone-weary. I was heart-broken. I could not conjure up spontaneous and ardent faith.

My decision about whether to trust God wasn't merely an exercise of cognition. I wasn't trying to pass some Sunday School pop quiz. I was trying to enter into truth that was large enough to hold my own frailty, vulnerability, and weak faith—a truth as deniable as it is definite. But how, worn out with tears and blood, in a place without words and without certainty, could I reach for that truth?

That night, I held to the reality of God's goodness and love by taking up the practices of the church. Specifically by taking up prayer, the liturgy of the hours.

For most of church history, Christians understood prayer not primarily as a means of self-expression or an individual conversation with the divine, but as an inherited way of approaching

God, a way to wade into the ongoing stream of the church's communion with him.[1] In that moment in the hospital, I was not trying to "express my faith," to announce my wavering devotion to a room full of busy nurses. Nor was I trying to call down (in the words of Richard Dawkins) my "sky fairy" to come save me.[2] Through prayer I dared to believe that God was in the midst of my chaos and pain, whatever was to come. I was reaching for a reality that was larger and more enduring than what I felt in the moment.

Every prayer I have ever prayed, from the most faithful to the least, has been in part a confession uttered in the Gospel of Mark: "I believe; help my unbelief" (Mark 9:24). That was my prayer as I repeated the well-worn words of Compline that night. And as countless nights before, the church, in the midst of my weakness, responded with her ancient voice: "Here are some words. Pray them. They are strong enough to hold you. These will help your unbelief."

Faith, I've come to believe, is more craft than feeling. And prayer is our chief practice in the craft.

This is not to say that a relationship with God is something we accomplish by effort, or that there's a hierarchy of Christian achievement where an elite group excels at faith like some excel at sewing or basketball. Grace is the first and last word of the Christian life, and all of us are desperately in need of mercy and are deeply loved.

Faith comes as a gift. And any artisan will tell you that there is something miraculous about their craft. Madeline L'Engle said that any good work of art is more and better than the artist. Shakespeare, she said, "wrote better than he could write; Bach composed more deeply, more truly than he knew; Rembrandt's brush put more of the human spirit on canvas than Rembrandt could comprehend."[3] A gardener cannot make daffodils grow, nor can a baker force the alchemic glory of yeast and sugar. And yet we are given means of grace that we can practice, whether we feel like it or not, and these carry us. Craftsmen—writers, brewers, dancers, potters—show up and work, and they participate in a mystery. They take up a craft, again and again, on bad days and good, waiting for a flash of mercy, a gift of grace.

In our deepest moments of anxiety and darkness, we enter into this craft of prayer, at times trembling and feeble. Most often, we take up prayer not out of triumphant victory or unimpeachable trust but because prayer shapes us; it works back on us to change who we are and what we believe. Patterns of prayer draw us out of ourselves, out of our own time-bound moment, into the long story of Christ's work in and through his people over time.[4]

> *Faith, I've come to believe, is more craft than feeling. And prayer is our chief practice in the craft.*

As I prayed that night, I wanted to believe the things I proclaimed: that God knew and loved me, that this terrible moment, too, would be redeemed. I believed it and I didn't. Reaching for this old prayer service was an act of hope that it would put me under the knife, work in me like surgery, set things right in my own heart. I may as well have said, "Compline. STAT."

1

Finding Compline

Nightfall

IT WAS A DARK YEAR IN EVERY SENSE. It began with the move from my sunny hometown, Austin, Texas, to Pittsburgh in early January. One week later, my dad, back in Texas, died in the middle of the night. Always towering and certain as a mountain on the horizon, he was suddenly gone.

A month later, I miscarried and hemorrhaged, and we prayed Compline in the ER.

Grief had compounded. I was homesick. The pain of losing my dad was seismic, still rattling like aftershocks. It was a bleak season—we named it, as a grim joke, the "Pitts-of-despair-burgh."

The next month we found out we were pregnant again. It felt like a miracle. But early on I began bleeding, and the pregnancy became complicated. I was put on "medically restricted activity." I couldn't stand for long periods, walk more than a couple blocks, or lift anything above ten pounds, which meant I couldn't lift my then four-year-old. As I spent hours sitting in bed each day, my mind grew dimmer and darker. The bleeding continued near-constantly for two months, with weekly trips to the hospital when it picked up so much that we worried I was miscarrying or in danger of another hemorrhage. In the end, in late July, early in my second trimester, we lost another baby, a son.

During that long year, as autumn brought darkening days and frost settled in, I was a priest who couldn't pray.

I didn't know how to approach God anymore. There were too many things to say, too many questions without answers. My depth of pain overshadowed my ability with words. And, more painfully, I couldn't pray because I wasn't sure how to trust God.

Martin Luther wrote about seasons of devastation of faith, when any naive confidence in the goodness of God withers. It's then that we meet what Luther calls "the left hand of God."[1] God becomes foreign to us, perplexing, perhaps even terrifying.

Adrift in the current of my own doubt and grief, I was flailing. If you ask my husband about 2017, he says simply, "What kept us alive was Compline."

✦ ✦ ✦

An Anglicization of *completorium*, or "completion," Compline is the last prayer office of the day. It's a prayer service designed for nighttime.[2]

Imagine a world without electric light, a world lit dimly by torch or candle, a world full of shadows lurking with unseen terrors, a world in which no one could be summoned when a thief broke in and no ambulance could be called, a world where wild animals hid in the darkness, where demons and ghosts and other creatures of the night were living possibilities for everyone. This is the context in which the Christian practice of nighttime prayers arose, and it shapes the emotional tenor of these prayers.

For much of history, night was simply terrifying.

Roger Ekirch begins his fascinating history of nighttime by saying, "It would be difficult to exaggerate the suspicion and insecurity bred by darkness."[3] In the eighteenth century, Edmund Burke said there was no other "idea so universally terrible in all times, and in all countries, as darkness."[4] Shakespeare's Lucrece famously laments the "comfort-killing night, image of hell."[5]

Nighttime is also a pregnant symbol in the Christian tradition. God made the night. In wisdom, God made things such that every day we face a time of darkness. Yet in Revelation we're told that at the end of all things, "night will be no more" (Revelation 22:5; cf. Isaiah 60:19). And Jesus himself is called a light in the darkness. He is the light that darkness cannot overcome.

The sixteenth-century Saint John of the Cross coined the phrase "the dark night of the soul" to refer to a time of grief, doubt, and spiritual crisis, when God seems shadowy and distant.[6] The reason this resonates with us is because night typifies our fears and doubts—"the hard day of the soul" or "the gray morning of the soul" would never have had the same staying power.

And in a darkness so complete that it's hard for us to now imagine, Christians rose from their beds and prayed vigils in the night. The third-century North African theologian Tertullian refers to "assemblies at night" in which families would rise from their sleep to pray together.[7] In the East, Basil the Great instructed Christians that "at the beginning of the night we ask that our rest be without offense . . . and at this hour also Psalm [91] must be recited."[8] Long after night vigils ceased to be a regular practice among families, monks continued to pray through the small hours, rising in the middle of the night to sing Psalms together, staving off the threat of darkness. Centuries of Christians have faced their fears of unknown dangers and confessed their own vulnerability each night, using the dependable words the church gave them to pray.

Of course, not all of us feel afraid at night. I have friends who relish nighttime—its stark beauty, its contemplative quiet, its space to think and pray.[9] Anne Brontë begins her poem "Night" declaring, "I love the silent hour of night."[10]

There is much to love about the night. Nightingale song and candlelight, the sparkling city or the crackling of a fire as stars slowly creep across the sky, the sun descending into the horizon silhouetting a reddened sky. Yet each of us begins to feel vulnerable if the darkness is too deep or lasts too long. It is in large part due to the presence of light that we can walk around without fear at night. With the flick of a switch, we can see as well as if we were in daylight. But go out into the woods or far from civilization, and we still feel the almost primordial sense of danger and helplessness that nighttime brings.

In deep darkness, even the strongest among us are small and defenseless.

Despite modernity's buzzing light bulbs and twenty-four-hour drive-throughs, we nonetheless face our vulnerability in a unique way as darkness falls. There's a reason horror movies are usually set at night. We still speak of the "witching hour." And poet John Rives, the curator of The Museum of Four in the Morning, a website that archives literary and pop culture references to 4 a.m., calls it the "worst possible hour of the day."[11] These wee hours, he says, are a popular shorthand infused with meaning across genres, cultures, and centuries.

Night is not just hours on the clock. How many of us lie awake at night, unable to fall back asleep, worrying over the day ahead, thinking of all that could go wrong, counting our sorrows?

Our very bodies confront darkness each night. So each night we practice facing our truest state: we are exposed, we cannot control our lives, we will die.

In the daylight, I'm distracted. At moments, even productive.

At night I feel alone, even in a house full of sleeping bodies. I feel small and mortal.

The darkness of nighttime amplifies grief and anxiety. I'm reminded with the setting of the sun that our days are numbered, and full of big and little losses.

We are all so very, very vulnerable.

We can speak of vulnerability as something we choose. We decide whether to "let ourselves" be vulnerable through sharing or withholding our truest selves—our stories, opinions, or feelings. In this sense, vulnerability means emotional exposure or honesty. But this isn't the kind of vulnerability I mean. Instead, I mean the unchosen vulnerability that we all carry, whether we admit it or not. The term *vulnerable* comes from a Latin word meaning "to wound."[12] We are

Every twenty-four hours, nighttime gives us a chance to practice embracing our own vulnerability.

wound-*able*. We can be hurt and destroyed, in body, mind, and soul. All of us, every last man, woman, and child, bear this kind of vulnerability till our dying day.

And every twenty-four hours, nighttime gives us a chance to practice embracing our own vulnerability.[13]

✦ ✦ ✦

I don't remember when I began praying Compline. It didn't begin dramatically. I'd heard Compline sung many times in darkened sanctuaries where I'd sneak in late and sit in silence, listening to prayers sung in perfect harmony.

In a home with two priests, copies of the Book of Common Prayer are everywhere, lying around like spare coasters. So one night, lost in the annals of forgotten nights, I picked it up and prayed Compline.

And then I kept doing it. I began praying Compline more often, barely registering it as any kind of new practice. It was just something I did, not every day, but a few nights a week, because I liked it. I found it beautiful and comforting.

A pattern of monastic prayer was largely set by Benedict and his monks in the sixth century. They prayed eight times a day: Matins (before dawn), Lauds (at sunrise), then Prime, Terce, Sext, None, and Vespers throughout the day (each about three hours apart). Finally, at bedtime, Compline.[14]

The Anglican Book of Common Prayer condensed these eight canonical hours into two prayer "offices," morning and evening prayer. But some Anglicans (as well as lay Roman Catholics, Lutherans, and others) continued to have fixed night prayers. Eventually, in Anglican prayer books these two prayer offices were expanded to four, adding vespers and a Compline service.[15]

Like most prayer offices, Compline includes a confession, a reading from the Psalms and other Scriptures, written and responsive prayers, and a time for silence or extemporaneous prayer.

For most of my life, I didn't know there were different kinds of prayer. Prayer meant one thing only: talking to God with words I came up with. Prayer was wordy, unscripted, self-expressive, spontaneous, and original. And I still pray this way, every day. "Free form" prayer is a good and indispensable way to pray.

But I've come to believe that in order to sustain faith over a lifetime, we need to learn different ways of praying. Prayer is a vast territory, with room for silence and shouting, for creativity and repetition, for original and received prayers, for imagination and reason.

I brought a friend to my Anglican church and she objected to how our liturgy contained (in her words) "other people's prayers." She felt that prayer should be an original expression of one's own thoughts, feelings, and needs. But over a lifetime the ardor of our belief will wax and wane. This is a normal part of the Christian life. Inherited prayers and practices of the church tether us to belief, far more securely than our own vacillating perspective or self-expression.

Prayer forms us. And different ways of prayer aid us just as different types of paint, canvas, color, and light aid a painter.

When I was a priest who could not pray, the prayer offices of the church were the ancient tool God used to teach me to pray again. Stanley Hauerwas explains his love for praying "other people's prayers": "Evangelicalism," he says, "is constantly under the burden of re-inventing the wheel and you just get tired." He calls himself an advocate for practicing prayer offices because,

> We don't have to make it up. We know we're going to say these prayers. We know we're going to join in reading of the psalm. We're going to have these Scripture readings. . . . There's much to be said for Christianity as repetition and I think evangelicalism doesn't have enough repetition in a way that will form Christians to survive in a world that constantly tempts us to always think we have to do something new.[16]

When we pray the prayers we've been given by the church—the prayers of the psalmist and the saints, the Lord's Prayer, the Daily Office—we pray beyond what we can know, believe, or drum up in ourselves. "Other people's prayers" discipled me; they taught me how to believe again. The sweep of church history exclaims *lex orandi, lex credendi*, that the law of prayer is the law of belief.[17] We come to God with our little belief, however fleeting and feeble, and in prayer we are taught to walk more deeply into truth.

When my strength waned and my words ran dry, I needed to fall into a way of belief that carried me. I needed other people's prayers.

> *When we pray the prayers we've been given by the church—the prayers of the psalmist and the saints, the Lord's Prayer, the Daily Office—we pray beyond what we can know, believe, or drum up in ourselves.*

✦ ✦ ✦

When my own dark night of the soul came in 2017, nighttime was terrifying. The stillness of night heightened my own sense of loneliness and weakness. Unlit hours brought a vacant space where there was nothing before me but my own fears and whispering doubts. I'd stare at the hard, undeniable facts that anyone I loved could die that night, and that everyone I love will die someday—facts we most often ignore so we can make it through the day intact.

So I'd fill the long hours of darkness with glowing screens, consuming mass amounts of articles and social media, binge-watching Netflix, and guzzling think pieces till I collapsed into a fitful sleep. When I tried to stop, I'd sit instead in the bare night, overwhelmed and afraid. Eventually I'd begin to cry and, feeling miserable, return to screens and distraction—because it was better than sadness. It felt easier, anyway. Less heavy.

The mechanics of my nightly internet consumption were the same as those of the addict: faced with grief and fear, I turned to something to numb myself. When I compulsively opened up my computer, I'd go for hours without thinking about death or my dad or miscarriages or homesickness or my confusion about God's presence in the midst of suffering.

I began seeing a counselor. When I told her about my sadness and anxiety at night, she challenged me to turn off digital devices and embrace what she called "comfort activities" each night—a long bath, a book, a glass of wine, prayer, silence, journaling maybe. No screens. I fell off the wagon probably a hundred times in as many days.

> I needed a comfort that looked unflinchingly at loss and death.

But slowly I started to return to Compline.

I needed words to contain my sadness and fear. I needed comfort, but I needed the sort of comfort that doesn't pretend that things are shiny or safe or right in the world. I needed a comfort that looked unflinchingly at loss and death. And Compline is rung round with death.

It begins "The Lord Almighty grant us a peaceful night and a perfect end." *A perfect end of what?* I'd think—*the day, the week? My life?* We pray, "Into your hands, O Lord, I commend my spirit"—the words Jesus spoke as he was dying. We pray, "Be our light in the darkness, O Lord, and in your great mercy defend us from all perils and dangers of this night," because we are admitting the thing that, left on my own, I go to great lengths to avoid facing: there are perils and dangers in the night. We end Compline by praying, "That awake we may watch with Christ, and asleep we may rest in peace." *Requiescat in pace.* RIP.

Compline speaks to God in the dark. And that's what I had to learn to do—to pray in the darkness of anxiety and vulnerability, in doubt and disillusionment. It was Compline that gave words to my anxiety and grief and allowed me to reencounter the doctrines of the church not as tidy little antidotes for pain, but as a light in darkness, as good news.

When we're drowning we need a lifeline, and our lifeline in grief cannot be mere optimism that maybe our circumstances will improve because we know that may not be true. We need practices that don't simply palliate our fears or pain, but that teach us to walk with God in the crucible of our own fragility.

During that difficult year, I didn't know how to hold to both God and the awful reality of human vulnerability. What I found was that it was the prayers and practices of the church that allowed me to hold to—or rather to be held by—God when little else seemed sturdy, to hold to the Christian story even when I found no satisfying answers.

There is one prayer in particular, toward the end of Compline, that came to contain my longing, pain, and hope. It's a prayer I've grown to love, that has come to feel somehow like part of my own body, a prayer we've prayed so often now as a family that my eight-year-old can rattle it off verbatim:

> Keep watch, dear Lord, with those who work, or watch, or weep this night, and give your angels charge over those who sleep. Tend the sick, Lord Christ; give rest to the

weary, bless the dying, soothe the suffering, pity the afflicted, shield the joyous; and all for your love's sake.
Amen.

This prayer is widely attributed to St. Augustine,[18] but he
almost certainly did not write it. It seems to suddenly appear
centuries after Augustine's death. A gift, silently passed into
tradition, that allowed one family at least to endure this glorious, heartbreaking mystery of faith for a little longer.

As I said this prayer each night, I saw faces. I would say "bless
the dying" and imagine the final moments of my father's life, or
my lost sons. I would pray that God would bless those who work
and remember the busy nurses who had surrounded me in the
hospital. I would say "shield the joyous" and think of my
daughters sleeping safely in their room, cuddled up with their
stuffed owl and flamingo. I'd say "soothe the suffering" and see
my mom, newly widowed and adrift in grief on the other side
of the country. I'd say "give rest to the weary" and trace the
worry lines on my husband's sleeping face. And I would think
of the collective sorrow of the world, which we all carry in big
and small ways—the horrors that take away our breath, and the
common, ordinary losses of all our lives.

Like a botanist listing different oak species along a trail, this
prayer lists specific categories of human vulnerability. Instead
of praying in general for the weak or needy, we pause before
particular lived realities, unique instances of mortality and
weakness, and invite God into each.

This book is a meditation on this beloved prayer. It's about
how to continue to walk the way of faith without denying the
darkness. It's about the terrible yet common suffering we each
shoulder, and what trusting God might mean in the midst of it.[19]

2

Keep Watch, Dear Lord

Pain and Presence

WHEN I WAS A CHILD, I was afraid of what lurks in the dark—monsters in the closet, ghostly sounds of branches scratching the roof, bad guys just beyond the door.

Back then, I could bolt from my bed and wedge myself between my sleeping mom and dad. But now that I'm the grown up with my own five-year-old who squirms her way into our bed each night, where is my safe place? Imagined monsters in the closet seem easier to hide from than the fear of cancer or the throb of disappointment or the loss of a job or the hard conversations that I replay in my mind or my uncertainty about how to parent my kids or live life well or trust God.

The band Over the Rhine has a song that asks, "Who will guard the door when I am sleeping?"[1] Each night I ask that question. Is anyone watching out for me?

What does it mean for God to keep watch with us?

✦ ✦ ✦

Amid thousands of forgotten sermons in my life, there is one sentence in one sermon that I'll never forget.

It was a gray Sunday morning when I was in college. A few months before, a three-year-old boy in our congregation had drowned. Our church was still staggered in grief as I sat listening to my pastor, Hunter, preach about trusting God. "You cannot trust God to keep bad things from happening to you," he said. I was dumbstruck.

What Hunter said is self-evident. Bad things happen all the time, and I knew that then as I do now. But what he said was also devastating. In some wordless place deep within, I had hoped that God would keep bad things from happening to me— that it was somehow his job to do so, that he owed me that much. The plain truth of what Hunter said stood before me, obvious and terrible.

Of course, God does keep many bad things from happening to us. We do not know all the unnoticed ways we've been spared some misery—the accidents we weren't in, the injuries we just avoided, the destructive relationships we never began, the diseases our white blood cells silently snuffed from our bodies unbeknownst to us.

But Hunter's point was that God does not keep all bad things from happening to us. He cannot be trusted to do that because he never made that promise. Doing so is, apparently, not his job. Our Creator lets us remain vulnerable.

> *But if God cannot be trusted to keep bad things from happening to us, how can he be trusted at all?*

But if God cannot be trusted to keep bad things from happening to us, how can he be trusted at all?

This was the question that I couldn't shake, the question that haunted the empty silence of the night.

In 2017, after months of talk about grief and loss, about my parents and my marriage, about body trauma and depression, about nighttime and "comfort activities," my counselor looked at me and asked, "Where is God in all of this?"

Could I believe that God cares about me when he doesn't stop bad things from happening? Could I trust him when I'm terrified that he will let me, or those I love, hurt? When I look across the immense collective sadness of the world, can I still know God as kind or loving? Is anyone looking out for us? Is anyone keeping watch?

The theological struggle I was facing has a long history and a name: theodicy.

Theodicy names the abstract "problem of pain"—the logical dilemma of how God can be good and all-powerful even as horrible things regularly happen in the world. And it also names the crisis of faith that often comes from an encounter with suffering.[2]

This wasn't the first time that I'd wrestled with theodicy. But our difficult year—and perhaps simply growing older—made unresolved questions return with a vengeance and howl through the long, dark night.

Theodicy is not merely a cold philosophical conundrum. It is the engine of our grimmest doubts. It can sometimes wither belief altogether. A recent survey showed that the most commonly stated reason for unbelief among Millennials and Gen Z-ers was that they "have a hard time believing that a good God would allow so much evil or suffering in the world."

This is an increasingly common struggle. More young people voice frustration and confusion about theodicy now than in the last several generations.[3] Many of those who walk into agnosticism or atheism do so not out of any reasoned proof (since there is no irrefutable proof for or against God's existence) but out of a deep sense that, if there is a God, he (or she or it) cannot be trusted. This is unbelief as protest.[4] In Samuel Beckett's play *Endgame*, his character Hamm rejects the existence of God with the quip, "The bastard! He doesn't exist!"[5]

If there is no God, the problem of pain vanishes. In his book *Unapologetic*, Francis Spufford points out that "in the absence of God, of course, there's still pain. But there's no problem. It's just what happens."[6] But, he says,

> Once the God of everything is there in the picture, and the physics and biology and history of the world become in some ultimate sense His responsibility, the lack of love and protection in the order of things begins to shriek out. . . . The only easy way out of the problem is to discard the expectation that causes the problem, by ditching the author Himself.[7]

If there is no God of love, questions about theodicy evaporate, but so does any redemptive meaning our pain might have, any transcendent story in which we might situate our suffering. More importantly, when we dispose of the problem of pain in this way, we face the "problem of goodness."[8] Philosopher Alasdair MacIntyre wrote that when we reject God to ease the tension that pain creates, goodness goes with it. To call something "good" without any overarching meaning is merely to say, "Hurrah for this!" or "I like this!," which is well enough, but it disregards our deep intuition that true beauty, kindness, gentleness, and wonder participate in and point to a real and ultimate foundation.[9]

If there is no one to keep watch with us, no one we can trust to look out for us in the night, then anything that happens, however good or bad, is sheer chaos, chance, and biological accident. But belief in a transcendent God means we are stuck with the problem of pain. So there are libraries of books seeking to answer the question of theodicy—responses and solutions offered by the hundreds, many of them very good and wise.

Yet despite all the ink spilled, we are not satisfied. Our questions persist.

Because ultimately theodicy is not a cosmic algebra equation, where we can simply solve for x. It is almost primordial. A scream. An ache. A protest from the depths of the human heart.[10]

Where are you, oh God? Is anyone watching out for us? Does anyone see? And tell us why! Why this evil, this heartbreak, this suffering?

I have come to see theodicy as an existential knife-fight between the reality of our own quaking vulnerability and our hope for a God who can be trusted.

At the end of the day—in my case, literally in the darkness of the night—the problem of theodicy cannot be answered. As Flannery O'Connor wrote, it is not "a problem to be solved, but a mystery to be endured."[11]

We sometimes talk about mystery as if it's a code to crack—as if the full sweep of knowledge is available to us, but we just haven't sussed it out yet. But true mystery invokes things that are fundamentally beyond our grasp. Mystery is an encounter with an unsearchable reality, an acknowledgement that the world crackles with possibility because it is steeped in the shocking and unpredictable presence of God. Avery Cardinal Dulles wrote that mysteries are "not fully intelligible to the finite mind," but that the reason for this is "not the poverty but the richness" of the mystery.[12]

One reason the problem of suffering cannot be answered tidily is that pain and brokenness are, at their roots, anti-rational. Christians understand evil and suffering to be forces of "anti-creation."[13] They don't fit in the realm of reason and order because they frustrate reason and disintegrate order. If there was a neat rationale for pain, it would necessarily fit somewhere in the order of the cosmos, an essential part of reality. But the early church's understanding of suffering and evil was that they were an absurd and inexplicable abnormality, a gross absence of the good and true.[14]

But secondly, and much more importantly, the problem of pain can't be adequately answered because we don't primarily want *an answer*. When all is said and done, we don't want God to simply explain himself, to give an account of how hurricanes or head colds fit into his overall redemptive plan. We want action. We want to see things made right.[15]

At its heart, theodicy is the longing for a God who notices our suffering, who cares enough to act, and who will make all things new. It is an ache that cannot be shaken, which we all share deep in our bones and carry with us every day—and every night.

In my favorite C. S. Lewis book, *Till We Have Faces*, the protagonist Orual writes a complaint against the gods. We hear her stories of suffering: being born ugly, losing her mother as a young child, finding her truest friend and deepest love—her little sister—only to lose her. Grief after grief is spelled out in bitter detail.

Orual demands an answer. She demands that the gods vindicate themselves.

In the final pages of the book, with her list of accusations still in hand, Orual meets God in a vision. She is transformed, and concludes her book with this: "I know now, Lord, why you utter no answer. You are yourself the answer. Before your face questions die away. What other answer would suffice? Only words, words; to be led out to battle against other words."[16]

In our deepest suffering, we do not simply want words to battle other words. We want things made right.

Christians have always known the reality of pain. They've lived through wars and plagues, without vaccines or modern medicine, when death was ever at the door, when suffering was rampant and unavoidable, when nights were horrifyingly dark. Yet, millions of the faithful have long held stubbornly to this antinomy: God is good and powerful, and terrible things regularly happen in the world.

The church has always known this paradox, but instead of resolving its tension, it has let it persist. We have left this chord humming in dissonance for thousands of years, always believing that it will only be resolved when God himself sounds the final consonant note.

My deepest question, *Where is God in all this?*, is an ache that I hope to endure until my longing meets its end. I want justice; I want resurrection; I want wholeness, wellness, and restoration. And I won't be fully satisfied until God—before whose face our questions die away—sets every last thing right.

But we're not there yet. We live in the meantime. And in this meantime, how can we endure such a mystery? How can we live as Christians in a world where children suffer, where marriages disintegrate, where injustice rages, where tyrants succeed, where we face frustration and futility, where we get sick, where we all eventually die? How do we trust a God who does not stop all this from happening? How do we dare ask him to keep watch?

✦ ✦ ✦

As a pastor, I've come to see that in the most vulnerable and human moments of our lives, doctrine is unavoidable. When all else gives way, all of us, from atheists to monks, fall back on what we believe about the world, about ourselves, and about God.

My friend Julie (Hunter's wife) is an artist. Her watercolors hang in my kitchen. Years ago, when her son was very young, he had to have surgery. Like any parents whose child is going under the knife, my friends were anxious. Before the nurses wheeled their infant son into the operating room, Julie looked at Hunter and said, "We have to decide right now whether or not God is good, because if we wait to determine that by the results of this surgery, we will always keep God on trial."

If the question of whether God is real or not—or of whether God is kind or indifferent or a bastard—is determined solely by the balance of joy and sorrow in our own lives or in the world, we will never be able to say anything about who God is or what God is like. The evidence is frankly inconclusive. If the story of my short life and feelings determine God's character, then he is Jekyll and Hyde. This way of approaching God becomes a never-ending game of poker. For every breathtaking splash of a whale's breach, I raise you a forest fire obliterating acre after acre. For every monarch migration, I raise you ticks spreading Lyme disease. For every mother enraptured by her child's first smile, there is another mother whose newborn struggles for his final breath. For every inspiring act of human goodness, there is another person scheming against the weak. In all our lives, from the happiest to the most tragic, the circumstantial evidence for God's goodness is divided. There is beauty and there is horror.

We cannot hold together human vulnerability and God's trustworthiness at the same time unless there is some certain sign that God loves us, that he isn't an absentee landlord or, worse, a monster. But we cannot divine such a sign from the circumstances of our lives or of the world. We have to decide what we believe about who God is and what he is like. We have to decide if anyone keeps watch with us. It is unavoidably—even irritatingly—a decision based on doctrine, the first principles we return to again and again, the story we define our lives by.

Francis Spufford writes, "We don't have an argument that solves the problem of the cruel world, but we have a story."[17] This is why, no matter what we claim to believe or disbelieve, what rises to the surface in our most vulnerable moments is inevitably the story on which we build our lives.

Christianity does not give us a concise explanation for vulnerability, loss, or pain, but it gives us a story—a real story in history. The *Catechism of the Catholic Church* states that, "There is not a single aspect of the Christian message that is not in part an answer to the question of evil [and human suffering]."[18] It takes the whole story of redemptive history to shape our questions about God's presence in the darkness. There may be no tidy solution to the problem of pain, but this is not because these questions are unimportant or, in a final sense, unanswerable. If there is anything remotely approaching a Christian answer to our questions about theodicy, the story is the answer.

When Julie sat in a hospital waiting room as surgeons carved her son's tender skin, she committed herself to deciding whether God could be trusted, regardless of the result of the surgery. She had to decide if she believed these claims that Christianity makes about God's goodness. She quit the poker game, folded her cards, and decided to trust a God who did not guarantee that bad things would not happen to her or her son.

> *If there is anything remotely approaching a Christian answer to our questions about theodicy, the story is the answer.*

But this was not an arbitrary decision; not a leap in the dark. She was not simply ratcheting herself up to affirm the goodness of God in spite of contrary evidence. She did look to evidence, though not the evidence of her life, nor the tally of the total amount of good in the world versus the total amount of evil. Instead, she looked at the life of Jesus. It's on this story that she anchored her decision about whether she would trust God, without knowing what would happen next.

The church has always proclaimed that if we want to see what God is like, we look at Jesus—a man "acquainted with sorrow" (Isaiah 53:3), no stranger to grief, a peasant craftsman who knew suffering, big and small, and died as a criminal, mostly alone.

Mysteriously, God does not take away our vulnerability. He enters into it.

Jesus left a place where there is no night to enter into our darkness. He met with blisters and indigestion, with fractured relationships and the death of friends, with an oppressive empire, the indignity of poverty, and the terror of violence. One night he sweat blood, asking the Father to spare him from agony, weeping in the lonely darkness while his friends fell asleep. He said, "Not my will, but yours, be done" (Luke 22:42), and soon afterward he was tortured to death.

God did not keep bad things from happening to God himself.

To look to Jesus is to know that our Creator has felt pain, has known trouble, and is well-acquainted with sorrow. But our hope in suffering is not merely to gaze on the biography of an ancient man frozen in the pages of the Bible. The story of the gospel is not a mere mantra or a relic of history. It is alive and ongoing. The work of Jesus continues, even now, in our everyday lives. So in hardship we do not look to Jesus solely as one who has been there before, once upon a time in a distant past. We find he is here with us, in the present tense. He participates in our suffering, even as—mysteriously—in our suffering we participate in the fullness of Christ's life.

But we cannot embrace the Christian story or Christ's ongoing presence in our lives by an act of sheer will or an exercise in cognition. Our hope in sorrow is not something we carry around as a brute fact or, worse, a pat answer. I do not come to trust the Christian story in the same way I trust that Lake Superior is the largest of the Great Lakes or that bread is made of yeast and flour. The story we live by is one that we somehow enter into—we discover our own small lives and stories in the larger story of God and his church.

We do that through the practices and prayers we receive from those who have gone before us. We take up and learn the craft of faith that allows us to know an actual, surprising, frustrating, and relentlessly merciful God. In the present tense.

Years ago, during a vacation in New Hampshire, Jonathan and I climbed Mount Washington, which is notorious for erratic weather. It can change from sunny and warm to snowing in a few hours. The wind is so strong that it once held the record for the fastest wind gust on earth. On our hike, we thought we might be blown off the mountain (we have no photos from that day in which my hair is not blown entirely across my face). And then there's the fog, which settles so deep and thick that hikers have gotten lost and died. So the good people of New Hampshire have made cairns along the trail: massive, towering rock structures that plot the course. When the fog descends and the weather is dangerous, hikers can make it to shelter at the bottom of the mountain or at the top by walking from cairn to cairn in the white out.

In times of deep darkness, the cairns that have kept me in the way of Jesus were the prayers and practices of the church.

When I could not pray, the church said, "Here are prayers." When I could not believe, the church said, "Come to the table and be fed." When I could not worship, the church sang over me the language of faith.

> In times of deep darkness, the cairns that have kept me in the way of Jesus were the prayers and practices of the church.

Inherited ways of prayer and worship—liturgical practices—are a way that the ancient church built cairns for us, to help us endure this mystery, to keep us on this path of faith, to guide us home.

Theodicy is in no way "solved" for me. It is not in fact solvable in the here and now. In many ways I am still wandering in the fog. But I have found cairns to follow, and they have guided many others in the midst of this crazy and unpredictable weather.

✦ ✦ ✦

I have a friend who is a textile artist. Among other things, she sews nautical flags because, besides the fact that they're gorgeous, there's an accidental poetry to them. According to Merritt Tierce, "There are forty flags in a complete set of international maritime signal flags—one for each letter of the English alphabet, one for each number, and four flags called substitutes, which perform special operations."[19]

Raised by themselves or in different combinations, the flags mean different things. White with a blue cross, followed by a flag divided into four colored triangles means *What is the wind doing?* Yellow and red triangles mean *Man overboard*. There are combinations for races and to warn about gales. Tierce writes,

> I wish we could fly such flags, we humans, ships unto ourselves, to communicate our states of balm or damage, our current headings, our desires and lacks. Maybe my friend's radio has gone out, but at least he could fly his small I-am-suffering-on-this-sunny-day flag and I could raise my I-will-take-a-walk-with-you-and-listen flag. We could see each other, understand, and act, without having to say all the words.[20]

These days, with radio and digital communication, satellites and GPS, ships still keep flags on board in case all else fails, but they rarely use them. Flags on ships are a bit like oxygen masks on planes: they're necessary when things go very badly wrong. If all you have left, drifting alone in the middle of the vast ocean, is a small square of flapping fabric calling for help, things are about as dire as they can be.

Now picture yourself in a boat, lost and afraid, adrift as the sun sets, with no way to contact anyone except for the flag you've been given for this very moment. You don't know what else to do, so you raise the flag—bright white with a red X.

And you see a ship, distant but drawing nearer. It hoists flags in response, a bright red diamond on a white field, followed by another made of two triangles, yellow and red, and then lastly a white trapezoid marked with a red circle.

This is the flag combination that my friend sewed to hang on her bedroom wall. It means *I will keep close to you during the night.*

When I was drifting in grief, not knowing what else to do, the prayers of the church, especially the prayers of Compline, became my flag to fly in the night.

The hope God offers us is this: he will keep close to us, even in darkness, in doubt, in fear and vulnerability. He does not promise to keep bad things from happening. He does not promise that night will not come, or that it will not be terrifying, or that we will immediately be tugged to shore.

He promises that we will not be left alone. He will keep watch with us in the night.

Spufford writes that, ultimately, "we don't ask for a creator who can explain himself. We ask for a friend in time of grief, a true judge in times of perplexity, a wider hope than we can manage in time of despair." If we suffer deeply, he says, there is no explanation, no reason, no answer that can ease our heartbreak. "The only comfort that can do anything—and probably the most it can do is help you endure, or if you cannot endure to fail and fold without wholly hating yourself—is the comfort of feeling yourself loved."[21]

In the end, that's what I needed to know.

Part Two

The Way of the Vulnerable

Deep into that darkness peering,
long I stood there wondering,
fearing, doubting . . .

EDGAR ALLAN POE

And since we live in present tense
The only hope of making sense
All depends on the source of light

FUGAZI, "CLOSED CAPTIONED"

3

Those Who Weep

Lament

SLEEPING, EATING, DANCING, having sex, watching TV, going to a bar, taking the subway, fretting, tweeting, bathing, reading.

Any of these may fill our nights.

Why then does this prayer ask that God keep watch with those who work or watch or weep, specifically? I really don't know. It's obviously not meant to sum up the whole scope of nighttime activities.

But these three words have shaped me, in all their alliterative glory. As I prayed this prayer night after night, *working*, *watching*, and *weeping* began to represent not only things we may do at night, but the way we move faithfully through a world where we are all so prone to harm. These words became the sturdy trellis upon which grew my understanding of how to endure this mystery of theodicy.

Jesus responded to darkness by working, watching, and weeping—and we join with him by taking up the same.

Let's begin with the last one: weeping.

✦ ✦ ✦

My life's adversity has been no more than the usual. My experiences of loss and sorrow are ordinary.

I could complain, of course (and I do sometimes). I have met disappointment and grief, even some trauma. I've been in and out of counselors' offices to deal with childhood pain and present disappointment.

But I also have an enormous amount to be grateful for. I grew up with parents who cared about me. I have a graduate degree. I've never wondered where my next meal will come from. I have children I adore. I am relatively healthy. I am loved by people I love. I have it good.

Even in the hard year of 2017, I knew that my sadness was not unusual. Nearly all of us will lose a parent at some point. About a quarter of pregnancies end in miscarriage. Most people have moved, been homesick, and felt lonely. Yet knowing these experiences are common doesn't lessen the pain of walking through them ourselves.

For most of my life, with my particular Texas upbringing and my own temperament, I thought that the goodness of my life deemed me unqualified to say much about grief. "It could be worse" was a family mantra. My father, who grew up poor and knew hardships I have not, would often say, "I was sad I had no shoes till I saw a man with no feet." Then he'd pause and smile and say, "So I took his shoes. He doesn't need 'em. He doesn't have feet!"

Dad would also say, "I've had worse cuts on my lip and just kept on a-whistling." This became legendary in our family. There was no injury too terrible to not invoke Dad's call to keep on "a-whistling." Broken bones. Accidents. Surgery. My father must have previously suffered untold lip trauma, because he'd had worse cuts on his lip than any wound we could present.

Walker Percy wrote that Southern culture was a kind of syncretism between Stoicism and Christianity.[1] And my parents could grin and bear it with the best of the Stoics.

I don't think this is all bad. In a culture that's increasingly committed to nursing every grievance, there's deep wisdom in being able to name what is right and whole about life, to keep moving forward despite obstacles, to have a wider perspective, to look hardship in the eye and laugh.

But the dark side of this resistance to grief is that we do not learn to grieve ordinary suffering and loss—the commonplace but nonetheless heavy burdens we each carry. As long as anyone had it worse (which is always), I felt I didn't have permission to be sad, to weep, to mourn.

For a long time, I thought the only people allowed to mourn—at least publicly, and without qualification—were those who faced unparalleled tragedy. The rest of us muddle through with our comparatively small sorrows. We keep whistling.

I also used to think of grief as a season, something tragic that you get through. People lose a loved one and then, for a year or two, they grieve.

Certainly there are particular seasons of deep grief. Grief is, in part, a response to acute loss in our life. There are times of mourning. But the way I understand grief has changed. I've come to also see grief as part of the everyday experience of being human in a world that is both good and cruel. In this sense, grief is a constant for us. It is a real and right response to our vulnerability.

> *I've come to see grief as part of the everyday experience of being human in a world that is both good and cruel.*

I no longer define grief simply as a response to tragedy. Grief is commonplace. All of us walk in grief every day, in one way or another. We bear pain and loss, small disappointments and agonizing memories.

I taste pangs of sorrow even when things are most happy. When my children chirpily crawl into my bed early in the morning and wrap their arms around me, I'm in brief bliss. But even then there's some part of my brain that glimpses the shadow side: "Hold on," it says. "This will only last a short season." The flowers fade, the grass withers. Everything you love is fleeting. I still find deep joy in these moments; vulnerability and loss don't extinguish that. I don't exactly feel that I'm grieving at all. And most often, I go on with my mundane day, barely registering sadness. I have to get up and help the kids get ready for school.

And yet grief is always there, lying silently in the corner of every room like some decrepit family pet.

Our bright and shining lives, our explosions of joy, good work, and love, are always silhouetted by the shadow of death. There are times when sorrow quickens and sharpens, towering and unavoidable, and times it recedes. But it remains the white noise of all of human experience.

As a priest, I see this every week. The amount of pain shouldered by even the seemingly happiest among us is enough to leave me reeling. I stand before the people in my church, and I know their stories. Here is a gorgeous woman who seems to have it all together. Her beloved son is an addict, and she lives with the knowledge that her love is not enough to rescue him. Here is a man whose family seems perfect. He still reels from the pain of a father he could never please. Here is a woman with an enviable career. She longs to have a child and has stopped counting how many miscarriages she's had. My congregation is beautiful and ordinary, but in that one room each Sunday there's enough sadness to make the heavens silent.

I know a spiritual director who begins each of her sessions with five to ten minutes of silence. Sitting in silence is a new experience for many, and she told me that during these few minutes nearly everyone with whom she meets begins to cry. Most often they don't have words to explain why, but in that empty stillness the muted sorrow that we each bear spills from their eyes.

Of course the ever-present reality of grief does not mean that we feel sad all the time. Grief is as much a part of us as our circulatory system or our middle name, but we are complex people and we can, and do, hold both joy and grief together because they both witness to things that are true. Thankfully, even in a wounded world, we still taste glory, adventure, exuberance, even euphoria.

So what must we do?

For one, we must learn to weep. This is not something that comes naturally for many of us. We have to let ourselves notice, admit, and experience sadness. And we resist this in all kinds of ways, as individuals, as a culture, and as a church.

This prayer from Compline doesn't allow us to ignore grief. It reminds us of those who weep, because we all know, deep down, that every night people are weeping—and on one night or another, each of us will too.

I had a friend whose family was falling apart. Always an optimist, he told me one day, "I'm willing to grieve, but not to feel sad anymore. I'm tired of feeling sad." I almost laughed—not at his tragedy, but because I identified with his sentiment.

We just don't want to feel sad. We'll do almost anything to avoid it. And if we must feel sad, we at least want our sadness to end when we see fit. We want grief to be a task we can complete; the oven timer of our soul dings and we're on to something else. But that isn't how grief works. We control it as much as we control the weather. It is not simply an intellectual activity, a cognitive recognition of loss. Feeling sadness is the cost of being emotionally alive. It's the cost, even, of holiness. Christians have to let ourselves be a people who mourn. It's part of the deal. It's a defining characteristic of those Jesus called "blessed."

Mary Allerton, a poet and a Puritan who sailed to America on the *Mayflower*, wrote a poem after she birthed a stillborn child. It begins,

There is no time to grieve now, there is no time.
There is only time for labor in the cold.[2]

Nearly four hundred years after Allerton wrote these words, I sat in my church office as a woman spoke to me about her own sorrow. "I am grieving, but I don't have time for grief," she said. "There's so much work to do. I have to keep going." The similarity struck me. Here were two women in completely different circumstances, four centuries apart, and without knowing it they said nearly the exact same words. They shared the same ache.

Most Americans have an inherited tendency to resist grief. It's in our national DNA; it's the water we swim in. The United States tends toward optimism and forward progress, busyness and productivity.[3] Getting on with it. We're taught in subtle ways that "there is no time for grief."

Henri Nouwen begins his book *A Letter of Consolation* with a story of the months after his mother's death, when he realized that he had filled his life with work and activity. He writes,

The busy . . . life certainly did not encourage me to listen to my own inner cries. But one day, when I paused for a while in my office between appointments, I suddenly realized that I had not shed a single tear before or after mother's death. At that moment I saw that the world had such a grasp on me that it did not allow me to fully experience even the most personal, the most intimate, and the most mysterious event of my life. It seemed as if the voices around me were saying, "You have to keep going. Life goes on; people die, but you must continue to live, to work, to struggle. The past cannot be recreated. Look at what is ahead." I was obedient to these voices. . . . But I knew then that this would not last if I really took my mother and myself seriously.[4]

Nouwen went to a monastery for six months, and in that season of stillness he would catch himself quietly weeping, even when he wasn't consciously thinking about his mother or any other loss. In prayer and slowness, something shook free in him.

After my dad died, I took one week off to travel back to Texas, seven days packed with gatherings and funeral preparation. Then I got right back to work, taking on extra speaking events and writing projects, throwing myself into our new parish ministry. In the slower nighttime hours, buried grief would demand a hearing, but I usually refused to listen. All this work and activity were respectable addictions that allowed me to avoid, like Nouwen, "my own inner cries."

But unless we make space for grief, we cannot know the depths of the love of God, the healing God wrings from pain, the way grieving yields wisdom, comfort, even joy.

If we do not make time for grief, it will not simply disappear. Grief is stubborn. It will make itself heard or we will die trying to silence it. If we don't face it directly it comes out sideways, in ways that aren't always recognizable as grief: explosive anger, uncontrollable anxiety, compulsive shallowness, brooding bitterness, unchecked addiction. Grief is a ghost that can't be put to rest until its purpose has been fulfilled.

For years, Jonathan lived with an almost constant low-grade current of anger. It has shaped him and our life together, the charged third rail of our home. When he began seeing our therapist, Ginger, his anger began to slowly slacken. All of us who are close to him saw he was clearly growing in depth. He's still a passionate guy, and he'd admit that even now he's not the paragon of serenity, but he is learning to be slow to anger.

Curiously, as his anger receded, he cried—at first almost all the time. It happened often enough and publicly enough that a kind woman in our church showed up one Sunday with a gift of handkerchiefs. This was a sign of healing. Ginger told us that

underneath anger is always fear or sadness or both. A backlog
of grief that had been long ignored was now demanding a
hearing. Jonathan was grieving buried losses, even wordless and
unknown pain. Anger had hardened over old wounds, infected
and scab-like, and he couldn't heal until he bled a little, so tears
ran like blood.

Now, though he cries less frequently, he cries more willingly.
His tears are closer to the surface. He has his gift of handkerchiefs after all.

There has been much discussion in the past few years about
our "outrage culture" and how it stifles dissent and leads to a
less gentle, more polarized society. The Christian response to a
culture of outrage must not be to mimic or perpetuate it, but we
also cannot simply condemn outrage in favor of some pure form
of enlightened logic that denies emotion altogether. There is,
truly, plenty to be upset about, plenty of loss to mourn, plenty
to lament. The church's prophetic witness to an outrage culture
is to be a people who know how to weep together at the pain
and injustice in the world (both past and present) and at the
reality of our own sin and brokenness. We must learn to listen
to the fear and sadness underneath the anger that people spew
through political vitriol and digital venom.

After the publication of my first book, which was about daily
life, I led workshops with people from around the country ex-
ploring the ways we spend our days—our time, work, habits,
and practices. I would also ask people what they habitually go
to when they feel anxious, lonely, or sad.

Again and again, I saw how we habituate ourselves to lap up
numbing distractions when we feel pain. Instead of sitting in
the discomfort of vulnerability, we run to alcohol, work, social
media, movies, entertainment, even political debate. None of
these are bad things in themselves. These people I talked to
aren't shooting heroin each time they've had a bad day. But,
nevertheless, they were saying to me in a hundred different
ways that "there is no time for grief."

If we don't want a culture of outrage, we can't only be a reasoned culture or a distracted culture or a numbed or busy culture. We must learn to be a lamenting culture.

As a church, we must learn to slow down and let emptiness remain unfilled. We must make time for grief.

✦ ✦ ✦

One of my favorite pictures of the people of God is found in a little-noticed passage from the book of Ezra. At the end of the Exile, the foundation of the temple was finally laid. There was a big celebration, as the people of Israel gathered to worship and to mark God's restoration. This was the moment they had waited for, the rock and mortar of their redemption. And yet, Ezra tells us, "Many of the older priests and Levites and family heads, who had seen the former temple, wept aloud when they saw the foundation of this temple being laid, while many others shouted for joy. No one could distinguish the sound of the shouts of joy from the sound of weeping, because the people made so much noise." (Ezra 3:12-13 NIV). Dignity be damned—these were people who knew how to celebrate and mourn their losses at the same time. Even in this moment of triumphant restoration a scar remained, and it was worth weeping over.

This is what life looks like until God sets things right, life in the meantime, in the already and not yet. We have seen the foundation of the temple laid—Paul actually calls Jesus "the foundation" (1 Corinthians 3:11). There is so much overwhelming beauty in this life of faith we've been given; there is almost unimaginable grace that we receive even on the most mundane day. And yet things are not made new yet. Loss is ever present. Beauty and pain are wrapped up together, impossible to pry apart. In Ezra, the response of the people of God was to admit all of it, to deny or denigrate none of it, to proclaim hope and loss both thoroughly true, so much so that no one could distinguish the shouts of joy from the wails of sorrow.

We cannot learn to do this on our own. We need communal Christian practices to teach us how to voice both the fullness of pain and the fullness of joy, without diminishing either one a hair's breadth. In her book *Mudhouse Sabbath*, Lauren Winner notes how Christians are often quick to proclaim resurrection and hope, which she applauds. But, she says, "What churches do less well is grieve. We lack a ritual for the long and tiring process that is sorrow and loss."[5] But to walk faithfully through this dark world, we need to grieve our losses, however tragic, however common. We need to weep with those who weep. Our task is to take up practices where we name, with utter honesty, the brokenness of the world and the promise of what's to come.

> *Our task is to take up practices where we name, with utter honesty, the brokenness of the world and the promise of what's to come.*

✦ ✦ ✦

The Psalms were the church's first prayer book. For the earliest Christian fathers and mothers, prayer was the recitation of the Psalms, in the same way that today's evangelical might assume that prayer is talking to God in our own words. In Robert Wilken's discussion of early church fathers, he said,

> Prayer comes first, because without regular and disciplined prayer there is no genuine spiritual life. And prayer for the monk means something very specific: reciting the strophes of the psalms. Left to our own thoughts and words prayer moves on the surface. The psalms loosened their tongues and gave them a language to read the book of the heart and to enter more deeply into conversation with God.[6]

We are all so laden with semiconscious resentments and suspicions, discordant desires and half-baked beliefs, that we need constant tutoring from the ancient church, our older brothers and sisters who can teach us to "read the book of the heart."[7]

By praying the Psalms year after year for millennia, in nearly every language and place on earth, the church learns to remain alive to every uncomfortable and complex human emotion. We learn to celebrate and we learn to lament. John Calvin called the Psalms "the anatomy of all the parts of the soul." He says there is no human emotion that "anyone finds in himself whose image is not reflected in this mirror. All the griefs, sorrows, fears, misgivings, hopes, cares, anxieties, in short all the disquieting emotions with which the minds of men are wont to be agitated, the Holy Spirit hath here pictured exactly."[8]

The Psalms are dramatic. And life—even ordinary life—is dramatic, drenched in meaning, full of glorious beauty and deep pain.

Philosopher D. C. Schindler called contemporary life a "flight from reality"—the attempt to buffer the self, through technology, ease, and distraction, from the sorrows and dilemmas of our lives.[9] We are tempted by nearly every current of culture to form our lives so that there is no time for grief, but only the dim hum of consumption, dulling our agony—but, with it, our joy, wonder, and longing. The Psalms call us back into the dramatic depths of reality.

Over time, the practice of praying the Psalms teaches us both to weep and to laugh—and it teaches us what to weep and laugh about. Theologian J. Todd Billings writes that Augustine saw the Psalms as "God's way of reshaping our desires and perceptions so that [we] learn to lament in the right things and take joy in the right things."[10]

Our emotions are good; they are gifts from God that point us to truth. Our emotions can also be wayward and self-serving. Prayer invites us to bring our whole selves—in all our glorious complexity—to God, who knows us better than we ever will.

Historically, the church saw the Psalms as medicinal.[11] They heal us. They teach us how to be fully human and fully alive. As a doctor prescribes amoxicillin for a sinus infection, the church fathers prescribed meditation on and repetition of specific psalms for specific spiritual ailments. Athanasius wrote that "whatever your particular need or trouble, from [the Psalms] you can select a form of words to fit it, so that you . . . learn the way to remedy your ill."[12]

✦ ✦ ✦

Psalms of lament—both communal and individual—are the most common type of psalm in the Psalter. They voice disappointment, anger, sadness, pain, deep confusion, and loss. If our gathered worship expresses only unadulterated trust, confidence, victory, and renewal, we are learning to be less honest with God than the Scriptures themselves are. As the first prayer book, the Psalms provide the pattern of prayer for all prayer books since, and its prayers are as varied and multidimensional as our human experience.

Lament is an expression of sorrow. To learn to lament is to learn to weep. But it is more than that. In the lament psalms, the psalmist holds God to God's own promises. Psalm 44, for example, begins in utter perplexity, reminding God how he has cared for his people in the past and asking him why he seems to no longer be of help:

> Rouse yourself!
> Do not reject us forever!
>   Why do you hide your face?
> Why do you forget our affliction and oppression?
>   (Psalm 44:23-24)

It is better to come to God with sharp words than to remain distant from him, never voicing our doubts and disappointments. Better to rage at the Creator than to smolder in polite devotion. God did not smite the psalmist. Through the Psalms, he dares us to speak to him bluntly.

Yet, to make things trickier, most of us not only live in a culture that has inoculated itself against lament, we also live in a culture where it's easy to assume we know better than God. We are taught in subtle ways that our feelings and experiences are the center of reality. This is cultivated in us in big and small ways every day. An advertisement for jeans blares from my radio, proclaiming, "I speak my truth in my Calvins." This constant messaging reduces us to mere agents of our own self-expression and curated identities—what we think, what we feel, what we want, and what we buy. We begin to approach God only to judge him and his actions according to our own preferences and little-t truth. We wait for God to convince us that he's a useful accessory in our own project of self-creation. In this way, so very subtly, we approach God not in honest lament but as unhappy customers. God isn't giving us what we want, he isn't taking away the pain of this world, and frankly he's so terribly slow. We are not pleased with the job God is doing, and the customer is always right.

These competing cultural impulses—to paper over pain through distraction or false piety on one hand, and to demand from God our own way and judge him by our own standards on the other—leave us in a bind. How do our honest doubts and grief not become a howling unbelief, a transactional sense that God owes us something, or a kind of consumeristic judgment of God's performance, as if we're giving the Creator of the cosmos a bad Yelp review?

> *How do our honest doubts and grief not become a kind of consumeristic judgment of God's performance, as if we're giving the Creator of the cosmos a bad Yelp review?*

But the psalms of lament do not simply vent our grievances against an underperforming God. Billings continues, "By the Spirit, we bring our anger, fear, and grief before God in order that we may be seen by God. And being seen by God leads to transformation."[13] Lament is not only an act of self-expression or exorcising pain: it forms and heals us. The Psalms express every human emotion, but, taken up again and again, they never simply leave us as we are. They are strong medicine. They change us. The transformation they effect isn't to turn our sadness into happiness; they don't take grieving people and make them annoyingly peppy and optimistic. They never say "Chin up" or "It's not so bad." Nor do they tell us why we suffer.[14] Instead they fix our vision on God's love for us, and teach us to locate our own pain and longing in God's eternal drama.[15] They form us into a people who can hold the depths of our sorrow with utter honesty even as we hold to the promises of God.

✦ ✦ ✦

The early church understood praying the Psalms as praying along with Christ himself. This was in part because Jesus prayed the Psalms.[16] A lot. He repeated them more than any other part of the Hebrew Scriptures. And as he was dying, the words of Psalm 22 were ready on his lips. These words of darkest pain were his own.

When we look to the life of Jesus, we see a man fully alive to both weeping and laughter, to pain and to joy. He drank both to the dregs. Straight, no chaser.

Jesus wept as one with hope, but his hope did not diminish his weeping. When his friend Lazarus died, Jesus knew that he was about to raise him to life again, but he still made time for grief. He wept.

Jesus also takes evil seriously. At his friend's tomb, he was not only mourning that Lazarus ceased breathing. He was peering into the deep darkness of what theologian Thomas Long has called "capital-D Death."[17] In that moment Jesus saw not only the physical end of a friend's life, but the entire reality of human suffering, the long night that all of us must endure in this lost and broken world. And he hated it. He hated Death—the power of sin and darkness in the world, the power of every big and little betrayal, the power of abuse, apathy, hatred, violence, genocide, and injustice.

Though Jesus raised his friend from the dead, it was not enough to quell the power of capital-D Death. Lazarus would still die. Lazarus would still live in an unkind world of grief, vulnerability, and disappointment. Jesus looked into that great darkness and he raged. He looked Death in the face and, "deeply moved" (John 11:38), he wept from the depths of his being. The Scriptures use a strange Greek phrase here that evokes the very undignified and gritty image of a horse snorting. Jesus' grief overflowed, something powerful and raw, almost animalistic.[18]

Jesus wept again as he sat gazing over the city of Jerusalem. Through tears he said, "How often would I have gathered your children together as a hen gathers her brood under her wings, and you were not willing!" (Matthew 23:37). Here he weeps not in rage at death, but in the sorrow of unrequited love. It's a deeply maternal image: Jesus longs to gather up children, wrap them up in the safety and intimacy of his embrace. But they refuse. Busy and distracted, the bustling city turns away. Any mother who has had to sit and watch her child destroy himself, watch her beloved walk into destruction, abuse, or addiction, watch as the one she sang over disappears into someone she cannot recognize, knows something about how Jesus wept over Jerusalem.

God himself took time to grieve. He is no stranger to the weight of heartbreak and horror, to the ache of swollen eyes that have cried so long they've run out of tears. He did not numb himself or downplay the losses. He never gave a pat answer. God was—and remains—shockingly emotionally alive.

✦ ✦ ✦

The end of the Bible turns to the end of time, and John describes a breathtaking moment when God will wipe every tear from his people's eyes (Revelation 21:4). When we finally see God face to face we will be made whole, and there will be no more death or crying or pain. All things will be set right. But—wait—not until we have one last, long cry.

Redemption itself does not skip over the darkness, but demands that every last tear run.

Christians believe that a place of eternal joy not only exists, but is more real than the diminished place of sorrow and pain we now know. The image of God wiping away our tears could of course be a metaphor—a statement that all things will, at last, be well. But what if it's not strictly poetic language? What if, in the face of our Maker, we get one last chance to honor all the losses this life has brought? What if we can stand before God someday and hear our life stories, told for the first time accurately and in their entirety, with all the twists and turns and meaning we couldn't follow when we lived through them? What if the story includes all the darkness of suffering, all the wounds we've received and given to others, all the horror of capital-D Death, and we get to weep one last time with God himself? What if before we begin to live in a world where all things are made new, we weep with the One who alone is able to permanently wipe away our tears?

4

Those Who Watch

Attention

THE DARKEST NIGHT I'VE EVER SEEN was during a summer in a remote village in western Uganda. The tiny town where we were staying had no electricity, so each night it was lit by small campfires. People gathered around them, talking and laughing; their faces flickered in the cheery light.

But one night was inexplicably still. Some fellow travelers and I left a missionary friend's house to walk about a quarter of a mile back to the school where we worked. That short walk felt like a lifetime. The pitch-black night held no moon or stars. I waved my hand an inch from my nose, and couldn't see it.

We lit a lantern and the four of us huddled around it—the only light for miles around. It illuminated about three steps of gravel road in front of us, then nothing for eternity. It felt like we might step off the edge of the earth. All was silent, save the eerie creak of the rusted lantern slightly swinging and the screams of bull-frogs in the night. I was terrified—afraid of the dark, afraid of what lay beyond the lantern light, afraid of all the things in heaven and earth that I could not see.

In the pitch-blackness, every sense was heightened. As best I could, I was keeping watch. I listened for every sound, my attention rapt. I noticed every shiver of the lantern's light, every bullfrog's bellow, every shuffle of my own soft steps. I was waiting to return to a safe place inside locked doors, or else for God-knows-what might meet us in the dark.

The next morning we learned that some of the guerrilla warfare from a conflict just across the border in Congo had spilled over into a deadly attack not far from us. The usual evening fires had been extinguished and everyone had sheltered inside their homes—except for us.

I will not soon forget that night or the forced concentration, the absorbing attention, that watching in pitch darkness can bring.

That quarter mile walk is how we live all our lives. We cannot see more than a few steps ahead. We do not know what the next hour, much less the next day, will bring. I felt vulnerable on that dark road, not because I was in greater danger than usual (I didn't know at the time about the violence happening nearby, and in fact no one came near us), but because I was in the dark, nearly alone, without the things I've come to rely on to make me feel secure and in control.

✦ ✦ ✦

In the relentless vulnerability of our lives, we not only weep—we watch.

C. S. Lewis said, "No one ever told me that grief felt so like fear."[1] Like Lewis, I find that my grief often shape-shifts into anxiety. The losses I've sustained make me afraid of what's ahead. I begin to think, "Not one more thing, Lord. Do not take away one more thing." But, of course, we can't make that bargain with God. We can scale the heights of human knowledge and still not know what will happen by breakfast time tomorrow.

Like a night watchman, we do not know which will come first, a criminal or the dawn. We resonate with the psalmist whose soul waits for God "more than watchmen for the morning" (Psalm 130:6). But our anxiety is that we have no idea when morning will come, or what will happen to us in the meantime.

We can only walk through life like I walked that gravel road, one step at a time, huddled together with our friends, clinging to the circle of light we've been given, and trusting God with what's beyond our sight.

As Christians, we take up watching as a practice—a task even. We stay on the lookout for grace.

We proclaim that even in the deepest darkness there is one we can trust, who will not leave us. We believe that even if the worst comes to pass there is a solidity to beauty, to God himself, that will remain.

Our posture of waiting does not deny the horrors of the night, but it bets on the morning to come.

Fear also keeps us on the lookout, but instead of dawn, we imagine only desolation. We assume there will not be grace enough for what lies ahead. Fear tells us there is no one with us who can be trusted on this dark road.

In this prayer of Compline, we pray for those who watch.

Sure, I take this literally—we are praying for late-night security guards, the police, firefighters, whoever eyes the military radar.

But when I pray this prayer, I'm also praying for those who wait and watch, not knowing what's to come. In this sense, all of us are "those who watch." If ever you've sat up at night, listening intently to the sound you aren't sure you heard, or to the fears in your own mind, then you know what it is to watch.

To watch is to wait. But to watch implies more than just waiting. It is not the bored malaise of standing in line at the DMV. It implies attention, yearning, and hope. It's the lover, flowers in hand, searching for that one face in a crowded airport, the expectant mother on alert for the first signs of labor, or the friend pacing outside the operating room.

The believer's constant posture is to lean slightly forward in anticipation. We wait for God to act, to set things right, to show up and work, whether that work is surprising and miraculous or a quiet change of tides.

We wait for God to bring healing to the sick, peace in our conflict, encouragement in disappointment, clarity in our befuddlement. And sometimes he does. And sometimes the sick die, the conflict worsens, the disappointment deepens, the confusion thickens. And yet we continue to watch and wait, knowing that the moment we can see—this small circle of lantern light—is not the whole road, not the whole story.

✦ ✦ ✦

Around a decade ago, my marriage was in a fragile place. Jonathan and I were both miserable, lonely, and weary from years of fighting. We had very young children and long lists of grievances and recriminations. So after months of counseling, we did the only thing we knew to do: we asked friends to pray, we dropped our kids off with Jonathan's mom, and we drove to Chattanooga, Tennessee. We hiked, and we ate great food. And we fought a lot, and cried, and talked and yelled, and hashed things out, then hiked some more, and yelled and talked and cried some more. In a gift store in Chattanooga, we found a magnet that now hangs on our fridge. It reads: "Everything will be okay in the end. If it's not okay, it's not the end."

We bought it as a statement on our marriage—we will work this out, we will listen, forgive, and learn to love, or we will die trying.[2] There was very little about our circumstances at the time that made us optimistic, but the promise of this magnet (however unintentionally) is not for this life only—it is eschatological. It expresses our hope that though "in the world [we] will have tribulation," Jesus has "overcome the world" (John 16:33); that as Julian of Norwich famously said, "All shall be well, all shall be well, and all manner of thing shall be well."[3]

But that doesn't mean things are well right now, or that we should pretend they are. It simply means that this is not the end.

I often focus on the this-worldly promises of the spiritual life: community, justice-seeking, spiritual formation. Yet if that's all that Christianity offers, it's at best a waste of time, and at worst oppressive and malicious, because walking in the way of Christ can make life harder, in the short-term anyway. The Christian story proclaims that our ultimate hope doesn't lie in our lifetime, in making life work for us on this side of the grave. We watch and wait for "the resurrection of the dead and the life of the world to come." God's promise to make all things new will not be fulfilled till God breaks into time, bearing eternity in his wake.

Christians believe that this cosmic reordering has already begun in the resurrection of Christ. Jesus' resurrection is the sole evidence that love triumphs over death, that beauty outlives horror, that the meek will inherit the earth, that those who mourn will be comforted. The reason I can continue watching and waiting, even as the world is shrouded in darkness, is because the things I long for are not rooted in wishful thinking or religious ritual but are as solid as a stone rolled away.

> *The reason I can continue watching and waiting, even as the world is shrouded in darkness, is because the things I long for are not rooted in wishful thinking or religious ritual but are as solid as a stone rolled away.*

When our lives are wrapped round with privilege and comfort, some may muse about the emotional benefit of spirituality or prayer—regardless of if what anyone believes is, strictly speaking, true. But when we're suffering it becomes clear that if there isn't a resurrection, we followers of Christ are wasting a lot of pain. It's when we encounter adversity that Paul's words make the most sense: "If in Christ we have hope in this life only, we are of all people most to be pitied" (1 Corinthians 15:19). It's ride or die.

It is because of Jesus' resurrection then that we can say "everything will be okay in the end." We endure the mystery of theodicy by waiting with bated breath for the things God has promised: for the kingdom to come, for peacemakers to be called God's children, for the pure of heart to see God, and for God himself to comfort us in our mourning.

My personal superheroes of attentiveness are birders.

The fervor with which true birders (or bird watchers)[4] pursue the golden-cheeked warbler or the whooping crane is inspiring, and more than a little eccentric. In the *New Yorker*, Jonathan Rosen describes birders as "genial caricatures of normal people." He continues, "As a birder myself, I recognize the symptoms: I've travelled great distances to see birds; I've totted up the names of birds on lists and felt weirdly comforted, as if they guarded me against oblivion; I've listened . . . to birdcalls on my iPod."[5]

My birder friends are masters of noticing. They study and catalog the natural world with a care and earnestness I scarcely have for anything. They notice the inhabitants of distant trees more than I notice what I'm wearing or who's sitting next to me on the bus. They're always on the lookout, and this startling attention reveals my inattention, how little I watch out for anything at all, how often I walk through a world of beauty and mercy and never look up.

There is an overlooked, workaday poetry in the little-known world of birders. Like all great poets, birders speak out of their profound observation of the world. They remind us that glory comes only by watching and waiting, by keeping an eye out for what most of us miss. Birdwatching websites and magazines are positively endearing to anyone who has ever been a jaded urban dweller. It's a breath of earnest fresh air. One birder's report reads: "The first species that I noticed tuning up this year was a tufted titmouse singing *Peter, Peter, Peter* in our orchard on a sunny Sunday afternoon in late January. His song was my first aural reminder that winter will eventually fade."[6]

If we have any hope at all, our hope is eschatological —that God will at last make this sad, old world new again.

Jesus is our first aural reminder that winter will fade. His resurrection is a real and fleshy promise.

But when Jesus ascended, he did not simply leave us with a token to remember him by until he returns. He promised to keep working. He sent his Holy Spirit to his people. The promise of the resurrection is also that Jesus is still at work today, in our own lives. In the present tense. So we wait and watch for the coming kingdom, when God will finally set things right, but we also wait and watch for glimpses of that kingdom here and now.

Prayer teaches us this craft of watching—not only for the eschaton but for God's work in our daily lives. Rowan Williams writes, "The experienced birdwatcher, sitting still, poised, alert, not tense or fussy, knows that this is the kind of place where something extraordinary suddenly bursts into view." He likens this to prayer: you sit still, waiting for glory, for grace, for God's presence. He writes, "Sometimes of course it means a long day sitting in the rain with nothing very much happening. I suspect that, for most of us, a lot of our experience of prayer is precisely that. . . . And I think that living in this sort of expectancy—living in awareness, your eyes sufficiently open and your mind both relaxed and attentive enough to see that when it happens—is basic to discipleship."[7]

Christian discipleship is a lifetime of training in how to pay attention to the right things, to notice God's work in our lives and in the world. Through long practice, we unfix our gaze from distractions and fears in order to attend to that which God attends. We learn to watch. Silence, stillness, and attentiveness are in short supply in our increasingly loud, digitized, and frenetic world. In his book *The Shallows*, Nicholas Carr shows how our brains are being physically rewired by our use of

technology so that we are more capable of taking in small, frag-
mentary snatches of information, but less capable of giving
sustained attention to any one person, argument, or experience.[8] Attentiveness is at critical risk of extinction.

The church's task is to learn to keep our eyes peeled for how
God is at work. We gather each week, watching for the coming
king. And with the earnestness of the Audubon society, we look
for the quiet, overlooked glory in our midst, for God's perplexing yet healing presence in the world. We watch for
glimpses of the redemption to come, even now. Through prayer,
through gathered worship, through the Scriptures and sacraments, we train our eyes to notice the light in the darkness.

✦ ✦ ✦

When Jesus himself sat under a darkened sky, he said this
same Compline petition, almost word for word. He asked his
friends to keep watch with him—to "keep watch with those
who watch."

On the night before he died, Jesus could taste the bitterness
of his utter vulnerability: "My soul is very sorrowful, even to
death" (Matthew 26:38). So he asked Peter, James, and John
to watch with him. Jesus was the man waiting for the verdict,
the woman waiting for the biopsy results, the mother waiting
for the surgeon to come back with an update. Jesus was waiting
for his "hour to come": he was waiting for his own death. And
with all the vulnerability of any other frail human, with puffy
eyes and a weary soul, he asked his friends to sit with him.

But his friends did not watch. They fell asleep.

So Jesus pleaded with them again, and this time the request
takes on a spiritual, even cosmic, urgency: "Watch and pray that
you may not enter into temptation" (Matthew 26:41). Now he
was not only asking that his friends wake up, he was calling them
to prayer, to *spiritual* alertness, to pay attention to true reality. He
was urging them to notice God's story unfolding in their midst.

And once again, his friends fell asleep.

This prayer I pray each night—that God would keep watch with those who watch—God himself prayed back to humanity, and we did not keep watch with him. But God showed grace for our weakness. He let his friends rest, and when the time came, he woke them up.

Jesus was left alone to pray, with tears and blood, through the long night. Because of this we can ask God to keep watch with us with full certainty that he will. He does not fall asleep.

Oliver O'Donovan points out that although the psalmists and the Old Testament prophets regularly call on God to wake up, this call is never sounded in the New Testament. God has already acted decisively through the incarnation, and the call is no longer that God would act. Jesus made it clear: God is with us, he knows our frailty and vulnerability as certainly as he knows the skin on his own hands.

The New Testament call is, instead, that we would stay awake to God, that we would be alert to God's work in the world. O'Donovan writes, "God has already awakened, has already acted. All that remains now is for [the faithful] to be awakened. . . . Addressed to believers, [the New Testament] stresses the need for continual alertness: 'Be awake! Stand firm!' (1 Corinthians 16:13), especially applied to persistence in prayer."[9]

Like James, John, and Peter, we are called to watch and to pray. Even, and perhaps especially, in seasons of darkness. I have learned that in the darkness I need to look out more intentionally for the Helper, for the ways God is actively noticing and loving us.

Just as our pupils dilate to let in more light, prayer adjusts our eyes to see God in the darkness.

I learn to do this through prayer. Just as our pupils dilate to let in more light, to see more than we first thought we could, prayer adjusts our eyes to see God in the darkness.

✦ ✦ ✦

Back in 2017, after a long time of avoidance and distraction, I slowly began to intentionally make space to weep and to watch. When I did, I began to intensely crave beauty and wonder.

The old saying is true: hunger is the best condiment. As I endured the mystery of loss, any picture of beauty, moral or physical, was like manna. On a walk one day, I noticed the specific color of yellow in a sunflower and I stopped and sat mesmerized—which, by the way, is not like me at all. The God who somehow allowed the bubonic plague also let sunflowers bloom in a shade of yellow that speaks only sublimity.

One week after my second miscarriage, I sat in silence, tears streaming down my eyes, watching the ocean and losing count of how many shades of green and blue I saw. Beauty itself was a mother to me, comforting me in her wordless embrace. And here's what struck me in that moment that made my tears run: there was no place she didn't go. There is no space on earth— no sadness too deep—that a verdant sprig of glory doesn't somehow crack through the sidewalk.

Beauty doesn't take away the pain of suffering or vulnerability. It's not like cicada song or good coffee make it hurt any less to lose a spouse or a friendship, or even just to have a hard day. But in the times when we think anguish and dimness are all there is in the world, that nothing is lovely or solid, beauty is a reminder that there is more to our stories than sin, pain, and death. There is eternal brilliance. It's not quite enough to resolve our questions or tie anything up in a nice metaphysical bow, but sometimes it is enough to get us through the next hour. And in enduring a mystery, we need just enough light to take one more step.

In the months after my two miscarriages, I still blessed and baptized babies. As a priest, it's part of the job. Some of my parishioners would apologize to me for this part of my work.

They worried it was salt in the wound to have to celebrate God's promises to other people's children while mourning the loss of my own. I appreciated their thoughtfulness, but for me it was just the opposite. I reveled in any hint that God was still at work, giving goodness to the world, bringing children to himself, birthing laughter. I needed to see that God was still present and active, that the church still bore witness to a love that was steadfast and enduring.

In those months, my daughters would often ask me to explain why miscarriages happen, and I'd tell them what my favorite doctor told me. "For a baby to be born, ten thousand things have to go just right." And I'd add, "But this also means that for you to be alive today, ten thousand things—and far more—went just right." This is a wonder that captured my imagination. I'd be in a crowd on the street or in church on Sunday and look at each face and think of the hundreds of thousands of things that had to go just right for us to be alive in the world, together on an ordinary day. The quotidian glory of all our lives is a gift. I lapped up wonder, attentive to any sign of life, any hint of comfort.

This wonder didn't diminish the pain one bit. But it did beget gratitude, which is just as real as grief.

But beauty and wonder were not only comforting. They were also a high-density dose of reality. The tenacity of glory and goodness, even in this shadowed world of tears, trains my eyes to pay attention, to stay alert not only to the darkness of our story, but to the light as well.

Simone Weil wrote that "absolutely unmixed attention is prayer."[10] Receiving the prayers of the church trains us in the way of unmixed attention. We learn to be people who take notice, who watch for God's grace to show up in our everyday lives. Christians, like all others, get busy and distracted. We fail to notice. Daily prayer has not made me float from spiritual bliss to spiritual bliss uninterrupted. But a regular practice of prayer corrects our vision over time. We learn to watch for what is all around us every minute—mercy, beauty, mystery, and a God who never ceases to wait and watch with us.

5

Those Who Work

Restoration

WE ARE DUST and to dust we shall return. But first, we work.

We leave our small mark on the world. For the most part it will soon be erased, as surely as my daughters' chalk drawings on the sidewalk will vanish with one hard rain. But our work matters, just as those chalked butterflies and rainbows matter to me and to my daughters. Our work—whether paid or not, drudgery or a joy, skilled or common—makes a difference. Done well, it adds truth, beauty, and goodness to the world. It pushes back the darkness.

Most of the prayers of Compline emerged before electricity and twenty-four-hour connectivity. When the world was lit by firelight, the majority of nighttime work was the work of crises—emergencies, grave illness, defense against intruders or armies. But that wasn't all the work done at night. From time to time, the poor and working class would rise midway through the night to relight fires or attend to other household tasks. The learned would study by flickering candlelight. Midwives guided new life into the world. Mothers woke to nurse or quiet their children. And monks would wake for their work of prayer.[1]

Our work weaves us together as a human race, dependent and interconnected. All of us rely on the work of others. We count on those who are often nameless and invisible to us. One Anglican night prayer reads: "Watch over those, both night and day, who work while others sleep, and grant that we may never forget that our common life depends upon each other's toil; through Jesus Christ our Lord."

Our life together depends on one another's toil. We need each other. We need others to do their work well.

One gift of vulnerability is that we are not sufficient alone. We wouldn't have made it past day one by ourselves. We are made to rely on others, and our ever-present neediness ensures that we must, whether we want to or not. None of us will ever be purely self-reliant. Bootstraps be damned.

Even before the first minor chord sounded in humanity's song, when things were as they should be and we knew no suffering or pain, we still were not self-sufficient. It was not good for man to be alone. In our purest humanity we were interdependent and needy. We relied on God and on other people. And we worked. We worked together even—our common life depended on each other's toil.

There are many paintings of Adam and Eve in a garden, blissful and naked, but very few portray them working in any way.[2] It's as if we can't imagine work without drudgery, as if paradise necessarily excludes office meetings and household chores (admittedly, Adam and Eve could skip out on laundry). But even in perfection, Adam and Eve worked.

We are made to share a common life of work and creativity. And once all things are redeemed, we will not suddenly become Supermen and Superwomen who are autonomous and self-sustaining. We will never not be needy. We will never not need God and one another. Our telos is community, not self-sufficiency. It's a feast, a life together.

Even now, we work toward this vision of redemption. We weep and watch, but we don't stop there. We don't take a passive posture toward the renewal of the world. Our shared human vulnerability calls us to action—to work. Our response to human vulnerability is always, in part, to seek to mitigate it, to make the world, however slightly, more peaceful, safe, beautiful, just, and truthful.

> *We don't take a passive posture toward redemption and renewal in the world. Our shared human vulnerability calls us to action—to work.*

Through our vocations, we seek to love others in embodied and practical ways. We do this through our jobs—the call to alleviate suffering births many of our vocations, from parenting to fighting fires to teaching yoga, from politics to medicine to social work. And we do this as a church. For two millennia, Christians have formed hospitals, orphanages, homes for the disabled and poor, schools and universities.[3] Beyond this, we care for those who are hurting in our daily life. We take care of one another in thousands of quiet, unsung ways. In 2017, church members showed up at my house bearing meals, art supplies for our kids, and, once, a big bottle of scotch. They helped shoulder our burden.

But good work in the darkness—in the face of our vulnerability and weakness—is not only done out of our desire to alleviate suffering. It also arises from our desire to defy it, to make beauty from ashes.

The week I found out my second son had died in utero, my close friend Katy was going to visit me from Nashville, to bring comfort and good conversation amid loss. But she had to cancel because she found out that same week that she had an aggressive form of cancer. I cried as I told my husband the news; he cried as he asked our daughters to pray for Katy.

After her diagnosis, Katy immediately entered into months of chemotherapy. And as life-saving poison pumped into her body, she wrote poems.[4] Katy is a poet, and the threat of death was not going to stop her from making beauty. Come hell or high water. Or chemo.

Her work was a way to form something luminous and enduring out of pain. In this way she would not let darkness have the last word. We work to bring justice to the world, to bring help in crisis, but we also work for beauty, laughter, and levity, for sheer pleasure. We paint, quilt, cook, act, and perform stand-up. All these kinds of work participate in God's mending of a world unraveled.

✦ ✦ ✦

As we pray for those who work, we hold two realities in tension; our own labor participates in God's work of bringing light into darkness, but all human work continues, in the meantime, in the midst of very real darkness.

We pray for those who work, and we know that work itself is often a place of futility, where we bump up against the wrecked state of the world. We experience what the Scriptures call "toil" (Ecclesiastes 2:17-26). We sow and seemingly do not reap. We fail.

The Scriptures constantly distinguish between the good work for which we are made and the presence of "toil" in our lives, the literal and metaphorical thorns and thistles that make work itself a place of pain. The Bible is full of lament over toil specifically— and nowhere more than Ecclesiastes. The writer of Ecclesiastes says he "hated life" because of toil (2:17), which is all "vanity and a chasing after the wind" (1:12–6:9). These verses won't make a good motivational poster for the wall of our cubicle, but the Scriptures do not mince words about the fact that our work is often disappointing, grueling, unrewarding, meaningless, and even exploitative and degrading.

A friend of mine whose husband has a seemingly great job in tech tells me that he often can't sleep at night because he's worried about his work. In his field, amid the dazzle of geniuses, startups, and youthful energy, people are expendable resources—a good quarter means new hires, a bad quarter means layoffs. Most of us work in industries where, in one way or another, our health, presence, home life, limits, and humanity are not valued.

Many of us lie awake anxiously, worried about our jobs. Still more are up late fretfully putting in a few more hours, trying to safeguard ourselves against our own dispensability.

But though each of us experiences toil, frustration, and futility in our work, clearly some have it harder than others—and these often work while the rest of us sleep. Though all sectors of society are increasingly working at night, the youngest, poorest, and least educated are far more likely to work through the dark hours. Immigrants in particular account for a disproportionate number of night-shift workers. The *Washington Post* explains that to be an immigrant in the United States frequently means "not only doing the jobs many Americans shun, but also working the hours many Americans won't."[5] When we pray for those who work at night, we are often praying for the poor, the marginalized, and the most vulnerable in our society.

In the eschatological reality we watch for, work itself will be made new. Isaiah 65 speaks of God creating a new heaven and new earth, where labor will no longer be marked by toil. It's not that we will no longer work—we won't spend eternity sitting around eating Cheetos and binging Netflix. Instead, God's people "shall long enjoy the work of their hands" (Isaiah 65:22). None of us will labor in vain. In *Signs Amid the Rubble*, Lesslie Newbigin writes that it is not only bodies that will one day be raised, but our work as well: "All the faithful labor of God's servants which time seems to have buried in the dust of failure, will be raised up, will be found to be there, transfigured, in the

new Kingdom. . . . Their labor was not lost, it has found its
place in the completed Kingdom."[6]

Our work was always meant to be a source of blessedness,
abundance, and joy that ripples through all eternity. As we
weep over the brokenness and futility of work, and watch for
God to restore all things, we also work, with whatever limited
gifts, influence, and capacity God has given us, for the renewal of work itself and of systems of labor and commerce in
our world.

✦ ✦ ✦

Prayer itself is a kind of work and it sends us into our work in
the world.

For the Christian, the postures of prayer and work are inter-
woven: *ora et labora*, pray and work. We work as prayer and pray
as work. And our prayer and our work transform each other.

Yet we can falsely pit prayer and work against each other, as
if one makes the other unnecessary. These days we tend to understand accomplishments as *either* our work or God's, but
never both.[7] We've come to subtly believe that our agency is
therefore in competition with God's agency. We believe the lie
that goodness, truth, beauty, healing, and justice are hewn
solely through our own effort or that they are God's to grant,
without any action on our part. God therefore is useful as a
miracle worker or a Hail Mary pass. He's a wizard we ask to zap
the world with signs and wonders when we aren't up for the job.
In this way of thinking, though we may sometimes call on God
to act when we're feeling desperate, we are mostly on our own.
In the warp and woof of life, in the laundry and law-making,
the finance and forestry, the medicine and mothering, the
ditch-digging and diplomacy, God is largely absent.

This kind of competitive agency is illustrated in a bit by
Scottish comedian Daniel Sloss (whose comedy I enjoy, despite
his metaphysics). Sloss talks about how disappointing it is for

parents to spend time, effort, and money on Christmas gifts
only for Santa to get all the credit. Then he says, "That's exactly how doctors feel whenever you thank God." He mimics a
cancer patient who goes into remission: "Oh, thank the Lord."
The doctor replies, "You know it's funny; I couldn't see his
name on your chart. Could see my name right at the top there:
Dr. Michaels." The patient argues, "The Lord sent you!" The
doctor replies (to the crowd's uproarious laughter), "He certainly didn't chip in for that medical degree." God gave the
cancer; the doctor cured it.[8]

If we accept the lens of competitive agency, God gets all the
blame and none of the credit. He is responsible for cancer, tsu-
namis, and car accidents while we deserve all the thanks for the
cure, the recovery effort, the safety engineering.

This way of understanding the world would have been unimaginable for most of human history. God's work was neither
understood as separate from nor in competition with our own;
it was the very life from which all fruitful work flows.[9] God did
not exist to fill in the gaps of what we cannot achieve through
our own work. The Christian understanding of agency is that
all good work is a participation in the very life of God. It is our
act of cooperation with the sustainer of the universe. It flows
from prayer and back into prayer.

The assumption of competitive agency affects all of us, even
Christians, so that we can sometimes come to see prayer as a
passive act. We are waiting for a breakthrough, for God to miraculously fix us. God may be a miracle worker, but he's a distant
one, showing up rarely and leaving the daily maintenance of
the world to us.

Or we reduce prayer to a personal moment of comfort or
piety. God is our pious pick-me-up, a break from the big bad
world of work, politics, and need.

Prayer then is either an escape, or a way to magically fill in
that small space where our own work fails.

But if God is behind, under, and throughout all good work and every moment of our lives, prayer is never a merely "spiritual" act of piety, a few feet off the ground, divorced from the real work of the world. When we pray for healing or redemption or peace or justice, we are praying for those who work—for scientists, doctors, poets, potters, researchers, retail clerks, farmers, politicians, and pilots—these actual and limited men and women through whom God is bringing renewal.

Praying this way changes how we work. We can take up our daily work knowing that through it we participate in the eternal work of God. We can take up our vocations not simply to find success, get a paycheck, or make a name for ourselves, but from a place of rest in God.

This view of work also changes prayer. The practice of prayer becomes a propulsive force, galvanizing our participation with God's work.

Harvard professor Steven Pinker's book *Enlightenment Now: The Case for Reason, Science, Humanism, and Progress* outlines how our lives have been improved by reason, particularly science and technology. Pinker explicitly pits prayer against this work of progress. He writes,

> Ever creative Homo Sapiens had long fought back against disease with quackery such as prayer. . . . But starting in the late 18th century with the invention of vaccination, and accelerating in the 19th century with acceptance of germ theory of disease, the tide of battle began to turn. Handwashing, midwifery, mosquito control, and especially the protection of drinking water by public sewerage and chlorinated tap water would come to save billions of lives.[10]

Pinker presumes that prayer—and God himself—dwells in some other dimension than handwashing, germ theory, or sewers. Believer and unbeliever alike can slip into this way of thinking. We wall off prayer, whether we think it's "quackery" or not, from hard human work, acts of genius, leaps in technology, or bills becoming laws.

One evening, I came downstairs and, to my surprise, found Jonathan crying while reading—positively weeping over the kindness and generosity of God. But he wasn't reading the Bible or the church fathers. He was reading Pinker's *Enlightenment Now*. I began to laugh. As my husband read about the billions of lives that have been saved through clean water and modern medical care, he saw the work of God in and through people's work. Steven Pinker and Jonathan were looking at the same data, but their stories about reality made them narrate that data in completely different ways. Where Pinker saw quackery, Jonathan saw glory. He was filled with wonder that God would usher such astounding healing into this sad world, and give men and women the privilege of participating in that work. The Christian story dares us to believe that the work of prayer is not so far away from the gift of sewers, that hands lifted in prayer and the scientific commendation of hand-washing flow from a shared source. Our work of prayer participates in and propels our public work of restoration.

> The Christian story dares us to believe that the work of prayer is not so far away from the gift of sewers.

I was a campus minister with graduate students and faculty for about a decade. I watched Christians who work in public health, research, literature, and the arts hold their work and worship together. Their very lives challenge any idea of competitive agency. One of my former students, a physicist, told me that she sees no conflict between her scientific research and the work of prayer, between what she named as "natural, observable cause and divine action." It brings joy, she says, that an unfathomable God chooses to do things in fathomable ways, ways we can learn about, grasp, and take part in.

One perk of serving as a priest in a parish near teaching hospitals and universities is that I regularly get a front row seat to watch some of the world's smartest people embrace prayer and redemptive work together. One friend and parishioner, Noel, has trained and studied for decades to be among a few dozen doctors in the United States who can do the kind of pediatric surgery he does. Sometimes his surgeries take over ten hours. They are complex, intense, and exhausting. And on those days, you can find Noel standing in a hospital break room, praying. Clipped to the door inside his surgical locker is a liturgy he prays before and during surgery. At the encouragement of his spiritual director, Noel wrote it himself, drawing from the Book of Common prayer and Scripture. He whispers: "Grant me, O Lord, for your sake, through the work of your Holy Spirit, love for my patient, joy in participating in this work, peace as I follow your lead, patience in the trying times of this case, kindness . . . to all in the room, goodness in this difficult task, faithfulness to have integrity in the details even when no one else but you sees . . . and self-control that my own sins of anger, anxiety, and vainglory would not mar my judgment." He prays for his patient by name. Then he scrubs back in and continues surgery.

His patients rave about him. One father says simply: "He saved my daughter's life." But Noel tells me his job is simply a chance to be "a minister of common grace." So as the sun sets at the end of a long day, he completes his work. A child has been helped and healed. And a man takes off his surgical mask and exhales a prayer of thanks that he could participate in God's restoration, that his work can be part of God's own work. My friend works as one who prays, and prays as one who works.

✦ ✦ ✦

Taken together, working and watching and weeping are a way to endure the mystery of theodicy. They are a faithful response to our shared human tragedy—but only when we hold all three *together*, giving space and energy to each, both as individuals and as a church.

If in the face of loss or failure, we launch immediately into work—into solutions, activity, programs, and plans—without leaving space for grief or attentiveness to God, our work will be compulsive, frenzied, and vain. (This is why, by the way, I reversed the prayer's order and began with weeping. Except in emergencies, there is usually wisdom in not going straight to work). If we watch for God's

> *Taken together, working and watching and weeping are a way to endure the mystery of theodicy. They are a faithful response to our shared human tragedy—but only when we hold all three together, giving space and energy to each, both as individuals and as a church.*

restoration without also mourning and laboring, we minimize the urgent needs of the world and become sentimental, apathetic, or passive. If we weep without watching for the coming kingdom and participating in God's work, we fall into despair. To take up the practices of weeping and watching compels us to work, and our work is shaped and sanctified by being people who, through embodied and habitual practices, have learned to weep and to watch.

✦ ✦ ✦

God entered this world of toil and did good work. Jesus wept, watched, and worked. He held all three together.

He healed people, and cast out demons. He alleviated suffering in this world. Not permanently—people still get sick. People still got sick even while he walked on earth. Francis Spufford points out that for all the healing Jesus accomplished, he barely moved the needle on the number of lepers in the ancient Near East or the number of women hemorrhaging or the number of people who died.[11] But through his work, Jesus showed us what the kingdom of God looks like: in the kingdom people are healed, forgiven, restored, and made whole.

Jesus also spent time—decades even—building stuff. Jesus was a tradesman. He is called a *tektōn* (Mark 6:3), a builder who used his hands. God came to earth and apparently thought it worth his while to take some wood or stone or metal and make something.[12] What did he make? We have no idea. Apparently nothing earth-shattering enough to have kept around. But in this dark world, where men and women were dying, where the poor were suffering, where injustice raged in a vast and violent empire, God became flesh and built some furniture. During all those decades that he spent building things, he wasn't preaching, healing, or clearing out temples. He wasn't starting a movement or raising the dead. The light came into the darkness and did ordinary work.

All of Jesus' work brought redemption. Not just the work that awed the crowds—the feeding of the multitude, the Sermon on the Mount, the raising of Jairus's daughter, but also his quiet craft.

The Gospels show us Jesus' rhythm of engaging in work and public ministry and then, as Luke says, "he would withdraw to desolate places and pray" (Luke 5:16). His work of prayer sent him out to his active life of work, which in turn sent him back into the work of prayer.

Jesus' work ultimately led him to the cross, where weeping, watching, and working meet.

On the cross, Jesus wept in darkness as he watched for a new world to be born, which he birthed through his own labor.

Even now, after his resurrection and ascension, God mysteriously continues weeping, watching, and working. The work of Jesus here on earth and his work now in heaven—which is not a far-off place, but nearer to us than our own bodies—is not completely dissimilar. His work in the incarnation and after his ascension are different, but they are not discordant. In his life on earth, we glimpse the continuing work of God even now.

At this very moment, Christ does the work of prayer, interceding for us.

He does not weep as we weep, but as our friend and Redeemer he enters into our weeping.

He watches with us, not as we watch, but in holy and perfect attentiveness, watching with utter and loving absorption as each sparrow falls, as each sea lily creeps across the ocean floor, as each mitochondrion gathers nutrients in our cells.

And he works to restore. In galaxies and empires, in our streets, homes, and offices, and in our beds at night, he works to make every last thing new.

Part Three

A Taxonomy of Vulnerability

*The world is indeed full of peril, and in it
there are many dark places; but still there
is much that is fair, and though in all
lands love is now mingled with grief,
it grows perhaps the greater.*

J. R. R. TOLKIEN, THE LORD OF THE RINGS

*Nighttime sharpens,
heightens each sensation.*

THE PHANTOM OF THE OPERA

6

Give Your Angels Charge Over Those Who Sleep

Cosmos and Commonplace

FOR ABOUT FIFTEEN YEARS, I forgot about the existence of angels.[1]

I didn't exactly decide I no longer believed in them, I simply didn't think about them, and if I ever did, it was a passing thought about how corny the depiction of angels usually is.

I rediscovered angels by putting a baby to sleep at night.

When my first child was a newborn, I realized one night, to my surprise, that without really noticing I had developed a habit of asking God to send his angels to protect her.

Back then I worked at Vanderbilt University, and became a regular at a Greek Orthodox cafe and bookstore near campus called the Alektor Café. I loved its quiet beauty, its ancient books, and its veggie chili. I got to know Fr. Parthenios, an Antiochian priest, and his wife (known to all as simply "Presbytera," or "priest's wife"), who ran the place together. One afternoon, late in my pregnancy, Presbytera handed me an icon of an angel and told me it was for the new baby. I appreciated her kindness, but wasn't particularly spiritually moved. I'm a Protestant, after all. At the time though I felt no particular skepticism toward either icons or angels, neither did I feel a deep connection to them. Still, I hung up the tiny wooden icon on my daughter's wall with a thumbtack.

Months later, as I prayed for my daughter before laying her in her crib each night, I would point out the icon and ask that angels would be near and protect her. I don't know what changed in my mind or heart. I don't understand how prayer about angels slowly bubbled up in me and suddenly seemed plausible and natural. My only explanation is that the towering responsibility—and love and vulnerability—of motherhood opened my heart to ask for help wherever it could be found. And there was the silent angel, looking strong and ancient, staring me and my daughter down each night as we sat in a darkened room. The practice of prayer, the kindness of Presbytera, and the still certainty of the icon conspired with my own maternal yearning to precede and shape my belief. My skepticism silently slipped away.

Parenthood brought a new level of anxiety. I keenly sensed my daughter's smallness and fragility in this giant cosmos, and knew that all the passion of my maternal love wasn't enough to keep her safe. I was small and fragile too. And yet, in our ordinary house in the vast darkness of night, I believed I wasn't alone.

This Compline prayer dares us to believe in a crowded cosmos.

None of us comes to what we believe by ourselves. The world has no free thinkers. Our imagination about who we are and what the universe is like is profoundly shaped by those around us and by the culture in which we live. After the Enlightenment in the West, our collective imagination emptied the cosmos of supernatural life, as sure as industry emptied Cape Cod of cod.[2]

Our default now, however subconsciously, is to imagine the cosmos as an empty sea on which we find ourselves drifting alone. Most of us who are educated into even mild sophistication—including Christians—proceed as if God is distant, as if the world is ours to control. It's not full of enchantment, not teeming with mysteries, and certainly not crawling with angels.

But this was not always the case. The historic church imagined a universe jam packed with angels, and ancient Christian leaders talk about angels a lot—more, frankly, than I am comfortable with. Aquinas called them "intellectual creatures" or "incorporeal creatures."[3] In the fifth century, Dionysius the Areopagite wrote, "Angels number a thousand times a thousand, ten thousand times ten thousand . . . so numerous indeed are the blessed armies of transcendent intelligent beings that they surpass the fragile and limited realm of our physical numbers."[4] Hilary of Poitiers wrote that "everything that seems empty is filled with the angels of God, and there is no place that is not inhabited by them as they go about their ministry."[5]

> *Our collective imagination emptied the cosmos of supernatural life, as sure as industry emptied Cape Cod of cod.*

I cannot even imagine living with this view of the universe, where you can spin around on an average day and bump into a thousand angels. What was assumed for centuries—that the universe is buzzing with divine life—is something I have to stretch to believe. Yet my ambivalence about angels is not due to reason. It stems from a failure of my imagination, an imagination formed by a disenchanted view of the world—the empty ocean of the cosmos. Even though I confess otherwise, I am often not particularly captured by any world beyond what I can see, hear, smell, taste, and touch. With this comes the loss of wonder. I rarely stop to consider that the universe—and even my small home—is drenched with the presence of God and full to the brim with spiritual mysteries. In his book *Recapturing the Wonder*, Mike Cosper writes, "Christians and non-Christians alike are disenchanted because we're all immersed in a world that presents a material understanding of reality as the plausible and grown-up way of thinking."[6]

Believing in the supernatural can frankly be a little embarrassing in my urban circles—especially the undignified supernatural. Not some vaguely exotic, hip new-age trend. But angels. Really? This is the stuff of cheesy figurines that line a batty aunt's bookshelves. In his introduction to *The Screwtape Letters*, C. S. Lewis wrote,

> In the plastic arts these symbols have steadily degenerated. Fra Angelico's angels carry in their face and gesture the peace and authority of heaven. Later come the chubby infantile nudes of Raphael; finally the soft, slim, girlish, and consolatory angels of nineteenth century art, shapes so feminine that they avoid being voluptuous only by their total insipidity.[7]

Between sweet little cherubs and Precious Moments and John Travolta dancing to Aretha Franklin in *Michael*, it wasn't that I rejected a belief in angels so much as that they were drained of reality. They had become silly, sentimentalized into parody.[8]

We Christians can be tempted to make our faith less enchanted. We try to prop it up with respectability. But the fact is, we still believe in a lot of weird stuff.

A few years ago, I heard an interview with the British theologian John Milbank in which he said, "I believe in all this fantastic stuff. I'm really bitterly opposed to . . . disenchantment in the modern churches, including I think among most modern evangelicals." He told a story about the Nottingham diocese in England, which he described as "a very evangelical diocese." They had received a request to participate in a radio show about angels. They surveyed their clergy, asking, "Is there anyone around who still believes in angels enough to talk about this?" Milbank chastised the diocese saying, "In my view, this is scandalous. They shouldn't even be ordained if they can't give a cogent account of the angelic and its place in the divine economy."[9] Milbank called for a re-enchantment of the church, that we should believe, confess, embrace, and admit all of Scripture and much of church tradition—even the weird stuff.

If we do not embrace an enchanted cosmos—the weird stuff—we miss the fullness of reality, the fullness of God, and we will never be able to embrace the mystery of our own lives, our tangled questions that will not find answers. To endure mystery, we have to learn to surf the teeming waves of wonder.

✦ ✦ ✦

Night is a time when we hear the whispers of a crowded cosmos and wonder about hidden spiritual realities. Our imaginations run wild with possibilities—every culture on earth is filled with stories of ghosts and other spirits that appear in the night.

This nighttime prayer calls us back to the supernatural. In it, we brush against the uncomfortable reality of a universe beyond what we can see, measure, or control.

Prayer itself, in any form, dares us to interact with a world beyond the material realm, a world filled with more mysteries than we can talk about in urbane company.

In one sense, prayer is completely ordinary. It's common and daily.

And yet it's a doorway into supernatural reality. Gussy prayer up as a moment of silence or wrap it round with scripted and beautiful words, but still, in a culture that imagines the world in only three dimensions, prayer is inevitably and blessedly undignified.

When I became a priest at a local church, supernatural phenomena became unavoidable. It's common for parishioners to approach a pastor on our staff asking for help with

an unexplainable spiritual encounter. And this isn't just batty
aunts. Physicians, professors, business people, who are apparently intelligent, well-adjusted, sane people ask if we could
maybe come pray at their home because they think they saw
a demon or had some other unexplainable experience. Eventually priests learn to respond to the supernatural like
plumbers respond to a call about a clogged drain. It's part of
the job. Every old priest I know has stories.

But it wasn't ultimately being a pastor or any odd experiences
that led me to a deeper belief in the supernatural. It was prayer.

Prayer expands our imagination about the nature of reality.

Cosper writes, "To come to live in the kingdom of God, or to
seek to live in a world other than our disenchanted milieu, requires a wholesale reordering of our habits and commitments."[10]
We are discipled by nearly every impulse of our culture to believe
that the here-and-now is all there is; that the only hope offered
for us is found in what we can taste, smell, feel, and see. To believe in something beyond the material world we have to take
up practices that form our imaginations—and hearts and
minds—in light of the resurrection, in light of the possibility
that, as Elizabeth Barrett Browning reminds us, "Earth's crammed
with heaven, and every common bush afire with God."[11]

Prayer often precedes belief.

Most popular understandings of prayer get this backwards.
We think of prayer as mostly self-expressive. In this way of
thinking, we begin with beliefs and feelings about God and the
world, and because of these, we learn to pray. Our prayers put
words to our inner life. But prayer actually shapes our inner life.
And if we pray the prayers we've been given, regardless of how
we feel about them or God at the time, we sometimes find, to
our surprise, that they teach us how to believe.

This is especially the case in times of suffering and sorrow.

When loss is acute, we often struggle to believe. Trusting God
feels like a steep climb. We are weary and our legs are shaky.

In times of deep pain in my own life, the belief of the church has carried me. When we confess the creeds in worship, we don't say, "I believe in God the Father . . ." because some weeks I do and some weeks, I can't climb that high. Instead we confess, "*We* believe . . ." Belief isn't a feeling inside of us, but a reality outside of us into which we enter, and when we find our faith faltering, sometimes all we can do is fall on the faith of the saints. We believe together. Thank God belief isn't left to me and my ever-fluctuating faithfulness.

In the midst of pain and doubt, "we need the guard rails of showing up for prayer and worship," explains philosopher James K. A. Smith. "There's going to be seasons in every Christian pilgrimage where you shouldn't be surprised to walk in that space. . . . Some days I show up at church with my doubts and I'm kind of counting on you to sing for me."[12]

The Scriptures, the songs, the sacraments, and the prayers of the church give us a lifeline in pain. When we want to know God but are too weak to walk, these practices carry us.

The universe has never been anything less than enchanted. We may cease to wonder at mysteries beyond our reach, but that doesn't diminish them one whit. The cosmos doesn't need our validation.

It is we who have been impoverished.

And yet we can never quite shake the sense that maybe—just maybe—there is more. We wonder if our ordinary lives are part of something unseen and holy, a grander story in which we might take our place.

The unseen is part of our experience of human vulnerability. We don't just feel vulnerable because we face loss, sickness, or death. We feel cosmically vulnerable. We feel our smallness in a vast universe. We sense that maybe there are forces of evil and good in the world that can't ever be proven or disproven under a microscope. We suspect on some deep-down level that there is more teeming in this vast ocean of reality than any of us imagine. And we wonder: if there is a supernatural reality, is it one of order or chaos? Of beauty or horror?

To know that you are not alone can be comforting or terrifying. On a dark night, when thunder roars and branches sway maniacally against our windows, my children are comforted when I tell them, "I'm here, you are not alone," because they trust me and love me. But the same idea can be the nightmarish twist of a horror film—"the call is coming from inside the house." Sensing that the world is crowded with mystery is a gift or a terror, depending on whether unseen things can be trusted or not. Does God come to us as a loving mother or as a stranger out to get us?

Prayer calls us into supernatural reality. And it also teaches us the nature of the God who governs both what is seen and unseen, the maker of aardvarks, angels, and who-knows-what-else.

✦ ✦ ✦

What I most love about this line—"and give your angels charge over those who sleep"—is that it pulls together supernatural cosmic strangeness and the most quotidian of human activities: sleeping.

We go to sleep each night in our ordinary beds in our ordinary homes in our ordinary lives. And we go to sleep in a universe filled to the brim with mystery and wonder. We always sleep in a crowded room in our crowded cosmos, so we ask for crazy things— that God send unimaginable supernatural beings to watch over us as we drool on our pillows.

> So we ask for crazy things—that God send unimaginable supernatural beings to watch over us as we drool on our pillows.

We are all helpless when we sleep. No matter how important our job is, no matter how impressive we may be, in order to live we all have to turn off and be unconscious for about a third of our lives.

Every day, whether we like it or not, we must enter into vulnerability in order to sleep. We can be harmed. We can be robbed. We can wake up in a new world of loss that we could not have imagined the night before.

We only want to sleep around those we trust because we know that in sleep we can be taken advantage of. We are at the mercy of those around us, and at the mercy of the night. We cannot protect ourselves from the towering terrors of violence or death, or the more mundane troubles of bad dreams and mosquitoes.

Sleep reminds us of our helplessness. Asleep, we have nothing to commend us; we accomplish nothing to put on our résumé. Because of this, sleep is a counter-formative practice that reminds us that our assurance is not the sum of our productivity, prowess, or power.

Or even in our ability to stay alive. In the Christian tradition, sleep has always been seen as a way we practice death. Both Jesus and Paul talk about death as a kind of sleep. Our nightly descent into unconsciousness is a daily memento mori, a reminder of our creatureliness, our limitations, and our weakness. When we go to sleep, we get as close as we who are alive and healthy come to the helplessness of death. And we do it every night.

Because sleep is so vulnerable, we sometimes have a hard time embracing it. We stay up late, staring at screens, working, or vegging out, lightbulbs buzzing softly into the night. We resist our bodily limits in every way we can.

But of course our bodies and brains are not inactive in sleep. There is a whole world of activity happening inside our heads. We dream. We fight illness. We form, sort, and strengthen memories from our days. Scientists tell us that learning actually happens in our sleep, and is even dependent on our sleep. Information that we take in during the day is subconsciously repeated again and again in our brains as we sleep so that we can absorb, remember, and integrate it into our lives.[13]

But the crucial part of all of this is that it happens completely without our knowledge, consent, or control. Our bodies are set up so that we have to loosen our grip on self-sufficiency and power if we are to thrive. Both physically and spiritually then, we must be willing to embrace vulnerability if we are to learn or grow at all.

> *Our bodies are set up so that we have to loosen our grip on self-sufficiency and power if we are to thrive.*

God designed the universe—and our bodies themselves—so that each day we must face the fact that we are not the stars on center stage. We are not the primary protagonist of the earth—or even of our own lives. Each night the revolution of planets, the activity of angels, and the work of God in the world goes on just fine without us. For the Christian, sleep is an embodied way to confess our trust that the work of God does not depend on us.

"Sleep is a perfect example of the combination of discipline and grace," writes James Bryan Smith. "You cannot make yourself sleep. You cannot force yourself to sleep. Sleep is an act of surrender. It is a declaration of trust, admitting that we are not God (who never sleeps), and that that is good news. We cannot make ourselves sleep, but we can create the conditions necessary for sleep."[14] To learn and to grow, quite literally, requires a posture of surrender.

✦ ✦ ✦

There are times when we cannot sleep because we feel so small. We are afraid of death, of failure, of being alone. We worry. These are the tender moments when our vast illusion that we're in control goes up in smoke.

Several years ago, my father had a massive heart attack on a cruise ship in the middle of the ocean. My brother, sister, and I got a message from our mom letting us know, but for a day or so we couldn't get any more information. Finally we got through to the ship's doctor and found out that Dad was going to be medically disembarked and transferred to a hospital in South America, but that the ship first had to sail all night to make it to shore. I remember lying in bed that night, thinking of my dad and mom rocking back and forth on a ship in the middle of the ocean. I could not save them, visit them, or even call them. I could not make the ship move any faster. I could not predict whether Dad would be alive in the morning. And with such a keen sense of my own powerlessness, I fell asleep quickly—something I rarely do.

Like a child who knows it's not her job to run the New York Stock Exchange since she can barely manage her times tables, the sense of how little I could control left me simply to relax into the care of God. This is not like me. Only when things got so far beyond what I could even pretend to manage did I remember I was not in charge of my life, or the lives of others.

Sleep is a daily, enfleshed reminder that it's God, not us, who is the maker and mover of all our lives.

Practices of prayer, like the practice of sleep, are a way to enter a posture of resting in God in the face of our utter frailty, with no promise of how or when morning will come. This is the ergonomics of salvation, the way we learn to walk in a world of darkness. And this posture of rest reshapes my continuing questions about how to trust a God who lets bad things happen. Cosper concludes,

> Our clawing, grasping attempts at answering every question and making sense of every mystery in life will end up in failure. Instead, God invites us to take a tour of the mad, mad world around us, to see ourselves as one mystery among the many, and to trust him that it all

makes sense in some strange, cosmic way. In doing so, we discover that the presence of mystery in the world is an invitation to wonder, and a world without mystery is a world of despair.[15]

There is more in heaven and earth than are dreamt of in our philosophy. There's a mad, mad world to tour, and we don't bear its weight on our shoulders. We are limited people, and there is more mystery in our own brains and bedrooms than we could ever pin down. And so we lay down and sleep each night knowing we aren't left alone.

Tend the Sick, Lord Christ

Embodiment

MORTALITY IS DOLED OUT in doses, from our first stuffy nose to our final demise.

We live each moment of our lives, from the best to the worst, in our bodies. We discover love not as an abstract idea, but by being fed and held close as infants. We know loneliness as a tightening ache just above our sternum. We meet the passing of seasons in an icy blast on our cheeks or hot pavement beneath our feet. Pain, pleasure, trauma, and anguish are embodied states. We do not simply have bodies; we are bodies. That's not all we are, but we are irreducibly embodied creatures. And when our bodies fall apart, so do we.

We get sick. We feel awful. Our thoughts grow fuzzy. We're tired and achy—or nauseated, in which case we feel almost nothing other than the pressing urgency of our gastrointestinal system. Human vulnerability is not merely an idea. It's as visceral as a sunburn or a scratchy throat.

In this part of this prayer, we aren't talking about dying—not yet. We're simply praying for the sick. And nighttime is particularly hard on the sick.

For starters, we feel worse as the sun sets. It's not just perception that makes it seem like we get sicker at night. Illness truly does peak at nighttime. Our immune systems have their own circadian rhythm, and the body's inflammation increases at night, which helps us toward healing.[1] But in the meantime, we feel miserable. (My kids' pediatrician tells me that children's bodies know the moment doctors' offices close, and wait till then to spike a fever.)

When I'm sick or caring for someone else who is sick, I dread nightfall. There's a distinct kind of exhausted anxiety that comes with taking care of a sick child through a long, dark night, counting the hours till morning. And when I am sick myself, darkness deepens my restlessness and loneliness. Sickness isolates us, and at night, when we can't sleep for all the coughing or vomiting or pain, we face unique misery, often alone.

We bear fragility in our very skin and cells, in large and small ways, so we pray for the sick. And what a huge range of people this is— we remember those with a common cold, but also cancer, a tangle with some past-date sushi, a case of Ebola.

> The church has long spoken about sickness as "death's handmaid," a practice drill for our inevitable decay.

Singer-songwriter David Wilcox has a brilliant little vignette where he describes a head cold as being "pulled over by the reaper for a warning."[2]

Sickness—like sleep, and like night itself—is another token of our mortality. The church has long spoken about sickness as "death's handmaid," a practice drill for our inevitable decay.[3] It is an unwanted reminder, however large or small, of our creaturely limits, our susceptibility to harm, our future undoing.

✦ ✦ ✦

The Latin word from which we get the word *human* (*humanus*) and the word for *earth* or *soil* (*humus*) spring from the same linguistic root. We are creatures of the dirt, of the dust.

The word *humility* also comes from this root. Sickness is in a very real sense humiliating. Our bodies remind us that we are all bubbling cauldrons of solids and liquids. We are not anywhere near invincible. We are born weak and we remain weak all our lives.

Headaches, nausea, vertigo, earaches—these reveal something true about us. Not only are we going to die someday, but even in the meantime we are limited. Our lives are bound by our flagging capacity. We are reminded in sickness that none of us is the master of our own destiny, the sustainer of our own life.

In 2017, when I was on "medically restricted activity" for months due to pregnancy complications, I couldn't go on a walk or shop for groceries or unpack our moving boxes. I felt like my body had blown a whistle and put me on the bench.

The requisite inactivity left me depressed. Sickness is boring. We were made to be well, to move, to run, to feel the wind on our faces, and when we are sidelined from all of this, our very body chemistry objects. We spiral quickly.

Sickness is also deeply frustrating. My body—which has brought me so much joy, which has let me birth babies and taste guacamole and swim in the frigid Irish Sea—now let me down. I have grown used to the great privilege of things inside my skin working correctly. I can achieve things. I can perform, meet expectations, check off my to-do list. And then suddenly I could not, and the obstacle was my own body. I had to cancel work events and ask friends to pick up my kids from school.

And when I could no longer achieve the things I wanted to, all I was left with was who I am, without adornment, without polish or productivity. Humiliating.

But this kind of humiliation humanizes us. Facing our frailty and limitations teaches us how to be human.

Our culture often resists this lesson. Weakness is not tolerated. In October 2019, Robert Half published an article called "Are Your Co-Workers Making You Sick?" At that time between 70 and 90 percent of Americans reported going to work sick. One-third of Americans said they never miss work for any reason, regardless of whatever havoc their bodies dish out.[4] And 55 percent of workers reported feeling guilty for calling in sick.[5] The majority of employees reported that they continue to work through illness because they have too much work to do to stay home. We are simply too busy to have bodies that falter. Human vulnerability, it turns out, is irritatingly inconvenient.

Employees also go to work sick because they don't have enough sick leave, or because their boss comes in sick and they want to measure up. We've created whole HR systems and corporate cultures based on our collective willingness to ignore the limits of our bodies.[6] But a resistance to the limits of embodiment only makes us sicker, both in body and soul. Not only do we spread our germs, but we spread an unhealthy habit of denying the reality of our weakness. If honoring our limits humanizes us, a culture that refuses limits is inherently dehumanizing.

We want to be indispensable, omnicompetent, and indestructible. But we are human, creatures of the dust. Embracing this truth about ourselves is the kind of humiliation that births freedom.

We come to know God when our ability to perform, to measure up, to achieve, fails us. Sickness dares us to embrace our belovedness, precisely because it undoes any illusion we have of our own invincibility and merit.

✦ ✦ ✦

The blessed humiliation of sickness is not only physical but also spiritual. Our illusions of piety can be undone with one toothache.

When our bodies give way, our wills do too. If habits of virtue—compassion, kindness, gentleness—haven't worked their way into us, if they haven't seeped into our very disposition, sickness exposes how very far we have to grow. When I feel sluggish or exhausted or feverish, I snap at my kids, I fall easily into despair, I throw bitter pity parties, I care very little about others. A lot of what appears as kindness or patience or holiness in my life is fueled by good health, energy, and simple pleasures. When these are taken away, it's clear that I am not that kind or patient after all. I just didn't have back pain.

> *It's clear that I am not that kind or patient after all. I just didn't have back pain.*

In Scott Cairns's *The End of Suffering*, he writes about a monk he met who was dying of cancer and told him, "Paradise is filled with men and women whose cancer saved their lives."[7]

It's not that cancer itself is anything to celebrate. Sickness is not the way things are supposed to be, and we don't have to pretend otherwise. But if we let it, our physical vulnerability can show us who we are and teach us to cry out to God (sometimes in moans, sometimes through vomiting). We find then that God meets us precisely when we have nothing to offer.

The historic church has called sickness an occasion—however uninvited—to grow in repentance and virtue. This is why an old monk can claim that cancer saves lives. This does not mean that sickness is a result of our sinfulness or that health is a result of our virtue, but that through this particular kind of embodied suffering we are made weak enough to be formed anew. The seventeenth century pastor Jeremy Taylor wrote, "There is nothing that can make sickness in any sense . . . tolerable, but only the grace of God: that . . . turns it into virtue."[8] God doesn't delight in sending cancer or canker sores, but the church has always said that sickness can be purifying because God meets us in the brokenness of our bodies, and puts even that brokenness to good use.

Cairns tells how, through cancer, his father grew from a man "prone to impatience" with a "considerable temper" to someone who was "remarkably calm, loving, and profoundly quiet—a genuine man of prayer."[9] His father died of cancer, but cancer saved his life.

I wonder if we might also meet this same grace in lesser crises. If cancer could save a life, can God be found among the more mundane miseries of sprained ankles and stomach bugs? Could these small "warnings from the reaper" not be mere tedium to be endured, the potholes in our well-paved roads of success and autonomy, but instead become a way our bodies tutor us in reality? Can our lungs and toes and wrinkles in-struct us in humanity and humility? We are frail. None of us are the sum of our achievements. All of us are creatures who stink and swell and wear out and are utterly loved. Knowing this brings freedom.

For nearly two decades, I've had chronic migraines.[10] I feel them come on, slow at first. A tired fogginess rolls in: an omen. Then the pain rises, sharp and icy. It seizes the right side of my body. Then nausea. I get hot, then teeth-chatteringly cold, then hot. I sweat and groan and collapse on the bed. Light stabs and sound roars, slamming against the inside of my skull. Pain drowns out all else. There have been years when my migraines quiet down. But there have also been years when they dom-inate the landscape of my life, disrupting my family and my work, rendering me mostly non-functional for a week or so each month.

For most of my life now, migraines have been a regular en-counter with an embodied theodicy—a way I run headlong (quite literally) into my own problem of pain. When I feel well, I do not ask God why he has allowed me to have migraines. I know that I can't know. But in the worst seasons of pain, I have moaned, "Why, Jesus? Why won't you take this away? Why can't I get better?" It's a howling at the moon, an animal yelping in a trap, pleading into a darkened sky.

But I can also say, without crossing my fingers, that there have been gifts that have come to me through this particular sickness. Chronic pain has connected me with my body and its rhythms and limits in a way I would never have learned otherwise. I love the world of ideas, and I can easily ignore my body altogether. But chronic pain has taught me to live in my skin and bones, with all the joy and sorrow that entails. I have had to learn to take care of my body. I've also had to learn to receive the care of others, which in turn has taught me to sit with others in their pain without trying to solve it. My chronic migraines are an ordinary, sometimes weekly, practice of sitting with God in literal darkness and pain.

But I have to be careful as I list these hidden blessings of chronic pain because, if I'm honest, it doesn't quite make it all worth it. If I could trade a little self-knowledge or empathy or connection to my body or to the mystery of suffering to have migraines disappear—and especially to have my husband and kids not have to deal with my illness—I would make that trade. But the Christian story dares me to believe that there is blessing in the fact that I don't decide these things. I do not determine the way of holiness or transformation for me (or for my husband and kids). We don't choose our preferred crosses, or our resurrections.

But I can only believe that it is good that I don't chart my life's path if I believe God himself is looking out for me in the midst of trouble. God is not a masochist who delights in our pain or weakness, but a cultivator whose grace is found even in the burn unit, the NICU, and the doctor's office. I can believe that God is good because God himself chose a way of suffering that none of us would ever choose—and he walked this way in a human body, as a creature of dust.

✦ ✦ ✦

If we want to grow in holiness, humility, and freedom, sickness is a willing tutor. Yet this kind of growth does not happen automatically. We have to learn, through long practice, to watch for God at work even in our faltering bodies.

Perhaps this is why in this prayer we ask God to "tend" the sick. We don't ask God to simply *heal* the sick—though we certainly pray for healing often in other prayers. Here we pray for tending.

Tending implies serving another, shepherding them, providing for their needs. It requires care, attention, and compassion. We want healing, of course, and we are told in Scripture to pray for healing (James 5:14). And tending certainly may involve healing. But we are asking for more here than for God to simply show up like a physician and make the sick well. This prayer has the audacity to ask that the God of the universe would stoop not only to heal us but to care for us, to nurse us in our most unimpressive states. We need God to bring wholeness to our souls, even through the brokenness of our bodies.

This prayer challenges us to believe that we need something even more than we need wellness. For God to take something as miserable and putrid as illness and make any beauty out of it, we need more than just healing. We need love.

The origin of the verb "to tend" and the adjective "tender" have the same Old French root, which means literally "to stretch." We are appealing to the tenderness of God—that the Creator of the universe would stretch to reach us even amid blood or snot or vomit.

When we're sick, we feel the waste of life in our aching bodies, the waste of the passing hours, the wasting away of our strength. Left on our own, that is all it would be: waste. But God lets nothing go to waste. We smell bad. We look terrible. Our very bodies have given out on us. We need tending. And

we have nothing to prove, nothing to measure up to, no performance necessary. We can allow God to tend us.

We receive our bodies as gifts from God. This can be hard for
us to believe if we spend our time counting their flaws, or ig-
noring them altogether.

Sickness reminds us how remarkable it is to have bodies that
work. In the gift of a body, we get so much more than we are
owed. We receive the privilege of walking, growing, eating,
aging, and laughing.

By adulthood most of us have gotten sick and then recovered
hundreds of times. Prayers for healing often come amid grave
disease and crises. But even healing from the small stuff—the
common cold or a splinter in our finger—is a marvel that involves multiple systems of our bodies in a delicate dance. And
it happens mostly without our conscious help.

I cannot remember all the thousands of times I've caught a
cold or burned my thumb on the stove or cut myself shaving,
which means I do not remember all the times I've been healed.
Each year of my life I've met with congestion and indigestion,
headaches and sinus infections. Each time, I've recovered.
And this gift of ordinary healing is so common that we barely
notice it.

Human bodies are glorious. The fact that our joints stay (for
the most part) well-oiled and our lungs keep breathing decade
after decade—for some of us, way past warranty—is a wonder,
a commonplace miracle. The human body is more spectacular
and intricate than anything else in the world. But we almost
never notice it. We take it for granted until it doesn't work.
Only then do we glimpse the kind of abundant mercy found on
an ordinary week with a functioning body.

Many of us—not all—have known moments when our
bodies worked just as they should. We've tasted the ocean on

our lips, known the rapture of a perfectly ripe peach, felt the happy soreness of summiting a mountain. Sickness, both slight and serious, is a diminishment of the glory for which we were made. The lush flavor of life replaced by the stale fluorescence of a hospital room or the dimness of a bleary day in bed.

So when we pray that God would tend the sick, we are praying that God will bring his tenderness, and even abundance, into this specific kind of human diminishment.

But when we pray for the sick we also remember the glory for which we are made. We recall that our health is a gift. It cannot be earned. It will not be constant. Any wellness we have will eventually give way. But we receive our bodies, day by day, with gratitude. In them we taste the fall, that things are broken and not yet made new. The reaper pulls us over for a warning.

But our bodies will be made eternal. They will rise from the dust in fleshy solidity, their glory permanently undiminished. So we also taste the promise of heaven in the goodness of our bodies. In this meantime, our flesh and blood is suspended between our defeat and our rescue, between fall and resurrection. We glimpse it all in our very cells. And in this tension and suspense, we learn to groan to God in our fragility, to lift trembling hands to God when we have no words, to meet God in our sinuses and skin. We learn to pray to the God who tends us.

8

Give Rest to the Weary

Weakness and Silence

WEARY IS A WEIGHTY WORD. It brings to mind heavy eyelids and aching joints, the worn out faces of those who have borne too much. To be truly weary is a state of both body and soul. The woman's swollen face after she's cried all that she can cry. The burned-out man collapsing on the couch after a brutal day. The couple who has gone round and round, circling the same impasse.

We know the difference between the kind of gratifying tiredness that comes after a good day's work and the burden of weariness, when the hardness of life settles on us thick and leaden. The book of Ecclesiastes names the latter the "weariness of the flesh" (Ecclesiastes 12:12). It comes with desolation, anxiety, and the deep sigh of despair.

In this prayer, we ask that God would give rest to the weary as Jesus promised that he would. In every Anglican prayer office, we read Scripture. In Compline, we read a quote from Jesus, when he spoke to a crowd and said, "Come to me, all you who are weary and burdened, and I will give you rest. Take my yoke upon you and learn from me, for I am gentle and humble in heart, and you will find rest for your souls. For my yoke is easy and my burden is light" (Matthew 11:28-30 NIV).

Jesus calls the weary to himself. He does not call the self-sufficient, nor those with the proper religious credentials or perfect, Instagram-able lives.

He calls those exhausted from toil, from just getting through the day. He calls those burdened with heavy loads, those weighed down by sin and sorrow. It is these, not the confident and successful, to whom Jesus says, "Come to me."

✦ ✦ ✦

One Ash Wednesday a decade ago, when I was new to Anglicanism, I knelt at a rail as Fr. Thomas, my priest, smeared a black cross on each forehead. "Remember that you are dust and to dust you shall return," he intoned, and marked the preteen girl kneeling next to me. Then, I heard her turn to her mom and whisper, "Does my ash look all right?"

Still kneeling, I started to laugh. Because of course it didn't look all right. She had a large black smudge in the middle of her forehead. There is no way for that to look all right.

But I also laughed because I heard my own heart in her question.

I know I'm limited. I know I'm dust and returning to dust. I bear vulnerability, weariness, and mortality. I bear sin, selfishness, and struggle. But I still want to, you know, look okay.

I'm a ten-year-old girl with a big, black smudge on my face hoping to somehow pass as acceptably cool.

I want to pretend I am still all right. I have it together. It's a well-practiced façade. I'm a ten-year-old girl with a big, black smudge on my face hoping to somehow pass as acceptably cool.

Though I love my church, for a while I hated my church's website and tried to keep its existence a complete secret (which defeats the point of having a website). My main complaint was that it said in giant letters on the home page: "We serve God with our strengths and find grace for our weaknesses." This is how we sometimes think about the Christian life. God smiles on our strengths, our competence, our capacity for goodness and beauty. And then, by grace, all our pesky imperfections are swept under the rug.

But the good news of Jesus is not that we get a merit badge for being put together and hope that God ignores our failures. We serve God not only with our strengths, but in our weaknesses.

God told Paul, "My grace is sufficient for you, for my power is made perfect in weakness" (2 Corinthians 12:9). And so Paul says that he will boast in his weaknesses. And then he all but loses it and says he will delight in weaknesses, in insults, in hardships, in persecutions, in difficulties, because it is in the very place of our weakness that God is strong. I wonder if Paul's website would say, "We serve God in our weaknesses and receive grace for all our damnable strengths."

In college, my best friend confessed his most secret sin to our pastor. Sitting on our pastor's deep-set porch, he told him what he was most ashamed of. Then my pastor said something that utterly transformed my friend: "We need you in our church, not in spite of your struggle, but because of it." The weakness and sin in my friend's life—and his ongoing story of repentance and becoming whole—was the very place where God could be most glimpsed and known, where God could show himself to the rest of us through my friend's life.

We come to church in the first place because we find ourselves to be needy. Rich Mullins wrote,

> I never understood why going to church made you a hypocrite . . . because nobody goes to church because they're perfect. If you've got it all together, you don't need to go. You can go jogging with all the other perfect people on Sunday morning. Every time you go to church, you're confessing again to yourself, to your family, to the people

you pass on the way there, to the people who will greet you that you don't have it all together. And that you need their support. You need their direction. You need some accountability; you need some help.[1]

The ones Jesus calls are the weary ones, the ones who snap at those they love after a long day, the ones who battle addiction, the ones who aren't who they wish they were, the ones who know they are not strong, the ones who wrestle and repent, who fail and fail again. This is the church, these ones through whom Jesus is strong.

To be clear, I don't mean that God is glorified in our fashionable weakness. It's a trend now to meticulously display imperfection online. Messiness can be part of our personal brand. We don't like people who seem too put together, so many Christian leaders are sure to go out of their way to show us how "messy" they are. But it's all so very curated. Our truest weaknesses will never be a selling point. It's those things that the people closest to us know about us that we'd rather forget—or perhaps that we don't even know about ourselves. It's those things we'd never share in a job interview and that people (we hope) won't mention in our eulogy.

One of my favorite movie lines is Lester Bangs's confession in *Almost Famous*: "The only true currency in this bankrupt world is what you share with someone else when you're uncool."[2] If sharing our imperfections makes us seem cooler and more approachable, then it's not true weakness. The things that are really wrong with us are embarrassing and uncomfortable. True vulnerability is too tender to trust with any except those who love us most. Sharing this part of ourselves with our community makes us more whole, but it will never help our brand. We are, truly, a mess—and not in a cute way, but in a sad and often humiliating way. The ashes on our forehead do not look all right.

No one can be really sick and truly cool at the same time. Ask any hospital nurse. The strongest among us are reduced to the neediness of babies when our health fails. In the same way, weariness, when it cuts us to the core, reveals our truest, most fragile selves.

Saint Isaac the Syrian said, "Blessed is the man who knows his own weakness, because awareness of this becomes the foundation and the beginning of all that is good and beautiful."[3] Our strength falters, and we grow weary. This experience of vulnerability can be painful, but if we embrace it, it is also salvific. Or rather, it can be the raw material God uses to bring us to the truth about who we are and who he is.

Oddly, when Jesus calls the weary to rest, he also calls them to a yoke—an instrument of work, not rest. It would have made more sense if Jesus had said, "I will give you rest. Take my warm blanket upon you." Or perhaps a pillow, or a bubble bath, or a day off. But Jesus offers the weary rest—and a yoke.

In the ancient Near East, it wasn't only animals who had yokes. Certain people would also carry yokes on their shoulders to bear heavy loads, their hands grasping chains or ropes to help them pull. But only the poorest people did this kind of work. Jesus is invoking a graphic image—a laborer sweating under the sun, neck muscles straining, their body nearly breaking under the load.[4] Jesus doesn't say that he'll exchange their yoke for a luxury condo or a vacation package. He offers his followers a different yoke—his. And he says that his yoke is easy and light.

A yoke represented rule or authority. To take on a yoke meant to submit to someone. In this passage, Jesus invites us to submit to his authority and "learn from him." In our weariness we are called to rest, but we are also called to learn, to be taught by one in authority. If we learn from the one who is "gentle and lowly," we will find rest for our souls.

There is no yokeless option. It seems to me the weary should be unyoked altogether, but instead Jesus suggests that all people are under a yoke, that it's impossible to not be yoked to someone or something.[5] It may be the yoke of religious law and scrupulous spirituality. It may be the yoke of our desires and passions, as raucous and exhausting as a newborn baby. It may be the yoke of cultural norms and assumptions, the water we swim in.

Jesus calls the weary not to follow their own way—that would be a heavy yoke indeed—but to submit to him and learn from him, to take on his yoke.

But why is Jesus' yoke light? Is it light because he promises that things will go well for us? That if we keep our side of the deal—if we're good boys and girls—he'll make our dreams come true and our life work out? That we'll have happy marriages? That we'll have children? That we'll find a vocation we enjoy? That we'll be healthy? That we'll be remembered when we die?

No. He calls us to an easy yoke, but he also calls us to take up our cross. How can the same person call us to both an easy yoke and a cross?

Jesus' yoke is light not because he promises ease or success, but because he promises to bear our burdens with us. He promises to shoulder our load.[6]

When I was a college student I met a missionary in Ireland who asked me a simple question that changed my life. I told her about my weariness, struggles, and doubt. She listened intently, and then asked me, "Is Jesus enough?"

If things didn't work out, if God seemed distant, if my life plans crumbled—was Jesus still enough? Or was I instead seeking Jesus *and* success, Jesus *and* happiness, Jesus *and* a fruitful ministry? Time and again in my life, when I face bitter disappointment, when I'm terrified of what's around the bend, when I fail, when I'm hurt by someone I trusted, when God isn't doing what I want him to do, I've had to return to that question.

Jesus promises nothing more or less than himself. He will yoke himself to us and never leave our side. He won't take away the weight we bear, but he will bear it with us. God owes us nothing. Any happiness, success, or desire fulfilled is a gift to be received gratefully. It's gravy.

God promises us simply himself. He refuses to be an end to any other means. By his mercy we can taste eternal life, which is defined by Scripture not as making it to heaven or seeing our dreams coming true or nothing bad ever happening, but as knowing the true God and the one he has sent (John 17:3). That's the promise: we can know God. Take it or leave it.

> *God promises us simply himself. He refuses to be an end to any other means.*

Is Jesus enough?

✦ ✦ ✦

If we delude ourselves that we can maintain a life of prayer by sheer effort and strength of will, weariness will inevitably puncture our inflated sense of self. The hardest time for me to pray is when I am weary. Spiritual discipline requires energy, and exhaustion turns resolution into dissipation.

When our strength evaporates, when we are spent, we often cannot drum up feelings of ardent faith or conjure the words for prayer. And this is why weariness is almost a prerequisite to learning to rest in God.

This is also why seasons of weariness taught me new and different ways to pray.

I have always loved words, so I have loved wordy prayers.

It wasn't until my late twenties, in a season of disappointment and heartache, when I ran out of words and slowly learned that there was more to prayer than I had known. I grew weary, my faith flagged, and I learned to receive the prayers of the church as my own. I learned that prayer is a tutor, not a performance. It's the stretcher on which we collapse and are carried to the Healer.

In 2017, I turned to Compline when I didn't have anything else to say, when I was so bone-tired and soul-spent that I could only receive prayer as a gift.

That year I also leaned on other ancient ways of praying that rely less on cognitive and verbal ability.

In particular, I found refuge in prayers of silence.

Theophan the Recluse, a nineteenth-century Russian Orthodox priest, describes the work of silent prayer: "You must descend from your head to your heart. . . . Whilst you are still in your head, thoughts will easily be subdued but will always be whirling about, like snow in winter or clouds of mosquitoes in the summer."[7] These clouds of mosquitos—my anger and neurosis, my fears and doubts, my unanswerable questions and exhaustion—buzz around me. Sitting wordlessly before God allows space for the real work to begin in my heart.

It's not that "Help" or "Lord, I'm weary" aren't good enough prayers. God hears and loves even prayers like these. We don't need to experiment with the prayers of the church or ancient prayer practices to impress God. But when we are weary, it can help to throw ourselves onto what has come before us, the steady practices of prayer that the church has handed down for safe keeping, for this very moment when we come to the end of ourselves.

In Christian spirituality, there are two ways to describe how we know God. One is kataphatic, "an active attempt to image God by the use of one's imagination and emotions."[8] Kataphatic spirituality is the way of energy—studying the Scriptures, learning theology, free prayer. It's a kind of athleticism of the Christian life, diligent and eager.

The other way is apophatic spirituality, which is quieter and less assertive. Bradley Holt writes in his book *Thirsty for God: A Brief History of Christian Spirituality* that apophatic spirituality strips "one's concept of God of all that is unworthy." It is the *via negativa*, or negative way of approaching God, learning who he is not, and it leads to "a state of utter passivity on the part of the mystic."[9]

I'm no mystic—I like margaritas and queso and sleeping in too much to ever be a mystic. But I have learned that when my strength is spent, I'm open to more passive and receptive kinds of prayer, which are not primarily led by my intellect or emotions. These ways of prayer teach me to rest in the ungraspable presence of God.

In 2017, I intensely craved silence—and yet I avoided it as well. I found prayers of silence alluring but also intimidating.

There is little that requires less of us than simply sitting in silence, doing nothing. It is prayer for the castaway who has forgotten the language of faith. In a sense, it's easy.

Yet sitting in silence is an exercise in tolerating mystery. It reminds us that there is a limit to the power of words and to human reason, even as a woman who loves words and argument.

> *Sitting in silence is an exercise in tolerating mystery.*

Silence gave me space to remember that my most urgent spiritual questions are not necessarily the ones that will endure. To be a Christian is to sit, however uncomfortably, in mystery, in something that we can never quite nail down or name. After all, we're talking about God here, the maker of the crab nebula and black holes and protons and puffins.

Silence also taught me to be patient with God's silence—to keep struggling to trust him when he wouldn't give an answer, a sign, or a quick resolution.

And when we are too weary to pray altogether, the one who knows our hearts far better than we do prays for us. "The Spirit helps us in our weakness," Paul writes. The Spirit of him who says "Come to me" comes to us. "For we do not know what to

pray for as we ought," Paul goes on, "but the Spirit himself intercedes for us with groanings too deep for words. And he who
searches hearts knows what is the mind of the Spirit, because
the Spirit intercedes for the saints according to the will of God"
(Romans 8:26-27). In our weakness, the Spirit of God does not
make us completely competent or all sufficient or winners in
life's lottery. Instead, he prays for us. God intercedes for us,
wordlessly. In our long, dark nights we don't know how to pray.
But we know God, the one who prays for us. And that is enough.

9

Bless the Dying

Ashes

THESE DAYS THERE ARE MANY who view the practice of prayer cynically: humans have a primitive fear of death and infinite darkness, so we invent a father figure or "sky fairy" to take care of us (provided we hold up our side of the bargain by living a moral life).

But here's where prayer gets interesting. The contemporary notion that prayer is nothing but an attempt to bargain with a fabricated god ignores the uncomfortable fact that Christians know, and always have known, that God doesn't sit around granting our every wish.[1] We ask for healing, happiness, and protection with full knowledge that, at least for now, God has nothing near a 100 percent track record for granting these requests. Every Christian on earth, if they live long enough, has a story about praying (and praying and praying) for someone to be healed or protected, only for the person to die anyway. If we're inventing a father figure or sky fairy who keeps us perfectly safe and fluffs our pillows each night, well, he sure isn't doing a great job at it.

In the service for the visitation of the sick in the 1549 *Book of Common Prayer*, the priest asks that Jesus would heal the sick person like he healed Peter's mother-in-law and Jairus's daughter. Then he suddenly pivots to make sure the sick person has made a will.[2] How's that for pragmatism?

Priests asked for healing in full faith that God can indeed heal, but in the sixteenth century lots of people who got sick died, so they covered all the bases. And this is in the official prayer book of the church. This wasn't the whispered doubts of skeptics, but our collective theological instruction: pray for miraculous healing, and get the will ready. It turns out that God hasn't been trusted to keep bad things from happening to us for generations upon generations. And yet generations upon generations have trusted God.

How can this be?

We don't pray the way people use magic. Prayer is not an incantation to wake a sleeping God. We pray as an act of hope in God's goodness. We pray because we believe that God, who makes no promises of our safety and comfort, loves us and takes care of us. We pray because our lives are part of the big story of God's work of redemption. And we pray to a Creator who has himself tasted death.

> *This wasn't the whispered doubts of skeptics, but our collective theological instruction: pray for miraculous healing, and get the will ready.*

✦ ✦ ✦

On Maundy Thursday, the Thursday of Holy Week, Anglicans gather to recall Jesus' last night on earth by washing each other's feet and receiving Communion.

At the end of the service, the priest strips the altar, removing everything that adorns it—the purple cloth, the linens, the candles—until the front of the church is blank. I've seen this done in different ways—solemnly, expressionlessly, mournfully, clumsily. My favorite was when my former pastor, who had a background in theater and a flair for the dramatic, would stomp up to the altar and rip off the altar cloths. He looked a little like a teenager being made to clean his room, or a fired employee emptying his desk.

He did this on purpose; the point was to treat holy things as if they were worthless; to approach the altar not in worship but in ire. The stripping of the altar transitions the church from the beauty of the Last Supper to the horrific suffering of Gethsemane and Good Friday. The holy Son of God was treated as worthless. He was stripped, beaten, and spat upon. We remember this and ransack the church of any sign of life.

We end Maundy Thursday in darkness. Any lights in the sanctuary are extinguished. Then, in the dark, someone reads Psalm 22: "My God, my God, why have you forsaken me? Why are you so far from saving me, from the words of my groaning?" And yet this Psalm, which weaves its way through so much torment—"I am a worm and not a man;" "Dogs encompass me, a company of evildoers encircles me; they have pierced my hands and feet"—ends in trust: "It shall be told of the Lord to the coming generation. They shall come and proclaim his righteousness to a people yet unborn, that he has done it!"

Jesus quoted this Psalm from the cross. And every year we sit before its words—Jesus' prayer and our prayer—with the altar stripped, in complete darkness.

In 2017 I preached at our Maundy Thursday service. Then I sat in a room adjacent to our sanctuary and wept, trying to stifle my sobs. I completely lost it. I worried I'd distract my parishioners, as they sat in contemplative silence trying to ignore the priest's muffled wails coming from the next room. My congregants see me cry in church all the time, but this was different—this was the guttural outpouring of raw grief.

My tears ran that night because the church had reminded me, through ritual, through the Psalm, and through darkness, that Jesus had experienced death. He knew what it was like to die. I did not.

The previous winter, night after night, I had wondered what it had been like for my father to die. I imagined his final moments again and again, more than I wanted to. I wondered whether he had known what was happening. He had told me that we'd talk the next day. Did he know that night was his last night? Was he afraid? Was he ready? Were there things he'd wished he had more time to say? Did death hurt? Did it feel like sleep, or a struggle? Did he see God? What could my dad see now, after death? What did he know or not know?

And what struck me, and brought both shock and comfort in its wake, was the realization that the God I worship knows exactly what death is like. He knows what death means for human beings. It's an experience God himself deigned to share with my dad, and with all of us. I have no idea what dying will be like—but Jesus does. He knows the feeling of his cells being starved of oxygen, of cardiac arrest and suffocation.

There is no darkness into which he has not descended. He knows the texture and taste of everything I most fear.

That Maundy Thursday the church sat with me in darkness, remembering the agony and abandonment of Jesus. Remembering his death.

✦ ✦ ✦

Ground zero of our human experience of vulnerability is the fact that we all will die, ourselves and everyone we love.

I utterly hate this.

One thing that draws me to Christianity is that we are allowed to hate death. I don't have to act as if the darkness is any less dark than it is. I don't have to stoically accept it as part of the circle of life. Death is an enemy.

In his book *The Doors of the Sea*, David Bentley Hart writes, "Our faith is in a God who has come to rescue his creation from the absurdity of sin, the emptiness and waste of death, the forces—whether calculating malevolence or imbecile chance

—that shatter living souls; and so we are permitted to hate these things with a perfect hatred."[3]

I love life in this world. The smell of lavender, the twang of a steel guitar, gathering clouds plump with rain. And our glorious bodies make all this enjoyment possible—these holy vessels allow us to taste salt and crunch fried chicken. To be alive is an irreducibly sensual experience.

The Christian faith never asks us to be okay with death. We are made to live, embodied and whole, to enjoy this wondrously sensual planet.

Whatever the metaphysics of death, there is a time when our bodies waste away. No more taste or smell or sound. But this is not the way it was supposed to be.

If we sentimentalize death and minimize its brutality, we end up, often unwittingly, belittling the hope of resurrection. The power of sin threatens to rob us of all that is lovely and bright in this world.

But God himself entered fully into frailty, lived in this world where things are decidedly not as they should be, and faced down the darkness of the grave.

Death is an enemy. But death is now an enemy defeated.

Christianity doesn't seem to mind paradox. Death is called "gain" by the apostle Paul (Philippians 1:21), in part because as long as capital-D Death—the curse of death and sin—is at work in the world, cessation of life can, at times, be a welcome release from suffering. I have known a few brave and faithful souls who were ready to go—who even asked us not to pray for their healing. They didn't know what death was like, but they knew in some mysterious way, that "to be absent from the body" is to "be present with the Lord" (2 Corinthians 5:8 KJV).

That we can be "present with the Lord" even as our bodies waste away is good news. But this is not our ultimate hope. Each week we proclaim in the Nicene Creed: "We look for the resurrection of the dead, and the life of the world to come."

Jesus takes care of his beloved ones in death, but death is not our friend, nor is it our ultimate destiny. It's not what we were made for. As N. T. Wright says, "Heaven is important, but it's not the end of the world."[4] In the end, we won't float off ephemerally into the by and by. We will see and know—even sensually know—this good old world made new. Through his resurrection, Jesus promises that everything we love in the world is lasting. We will taste and smell and feel and touch any and everything that God has called good.

✦ ✦ ✦

Every night as we lay down, comfortable in our warm beds, someone is dying. So as night falls, we remember them.

This part of the prayer became especially important to me after my dad's death. Because one night I went to sleep and the next morning when I woke up, my father was no longer here. Just one sleep can lead to a new and frightening world that we do not recognize. That night my father was dying, God knew that. I didn't.

So when I say "bless the dying," I'm well aware that I don't know who I am praying for. It could be any of us. We are all "the dying."

But what intrigues me about this prayer is not that it acknowledges the plain fact of death. It's that we ask God to "bless" the dying. This is never a prayer I'd get to on my own. This is the kind of paradigm shift that's only available when I let the church tell me how to pray. On my own, I would pray "save the dying." Or "help the dying." Certainly "stop the dying from dying." Maybe, if it comes to it, "raise the dying." But "bless" the dying? What could that mean? We're talking about people

> My own confusion shows me that I not only know very little about dying, I also know very little about blessing.

who are dying! What kind of blessing would suffice? And here my own confusion shows me that I not only know very little about dying, I also know very little about blessing.

The word *blessed* is cheapened in our day. We are #*blessed* by a new car or an expensive purse. Or perhaps by a job promotion, a marriage, or the birth of a new baby. These are blessings for which we are grateful. But how do any of these help us when we're dying? Death reveals the futility of much of what we chase in life. It exposes any anemic understanding of blessing.

In Scripture, the word *blessed* is used to describe those who are poor, who mourn, hunger, risk peace, or are persecuted (Matthew 5:3-12). These depths of human vulnerability birth a particular kind of blessedness. What does it mean to find blessing in the darkest moments of our lives? What would it mean for God to answer our prayer and bless the dying?

We are topsy-turvy. We don't know what's best for us. The things I'm most afraid of are often the very things that will set me free. The desolate places in my life that I most want to avoid are the very places God waits to meet me. The things I want most—and which I grip, white knuckled—are often the things that, were it not for God's gracious intervention, would diminish me, even kill me. The way to save my life is to lose it.

Many of us have heard this again and again, but to believe it is to retrain our minds that up is down and down is up. It goes completely against what feels natural because most often self-preservation, if not self-worship, is what feels most natural.

To trust God in our vulnerability is to willingly enter a lifelong exercise in becoming attuned to what blessing truly is, and how it is often found in the last place we'd look for it. The word for "blessed" in Jesus' Sermon on the Mount is *makarios*, which biblical scholar Jonathan Pennington translates "flourishing."[5] Flourishing are those who mourn. Flourishing are the poor in spirit. Flourishing are the meek. My vision of human flourishing, which I've been trained in from birth by thousands of advertisements and celebrity endorsements, is certainly not marked by mourning, meekness, poverty, or persecution.

Pennington goes on to show how Jesus embodies each beatitude.[6] If you want to see what human flourishing—what blessing—looks like, look no further than Jesus, our man of sorrows. He lived an uncomfortable life in poverty, never married or had sex, and died in pain, abandoned by his friends, in relative obscurity. Here is the arresting picture of the Blessed One, God's Anointed. To know Jesus is to learn to walk his strange path of flourishing, of abundant life.

We are always somewhere in between the stripped altar of Maundy Thursday and the glory of Easter bells. Our existence is irreducibly a life and death situation. We taste all of it: celebration and loss, the kindness and betrayal of those we love, the sweetness and the sadness, beauty and ashes.

Christian teaching and practice calls us into a life and death story—a story we ourselves did not write. So when we ask God to bless the dying, we are leaving it up to God to decide what that might look like. Of course blessing might mean that the dying are made well. But it might also mean that they die well—that their death, like their life, might be part of God's beautiful story, and that even in their dying moments they might find flourishing.

✦ ✦ ✦

Jaroslav Pelikan said that "Christ comes into the world to teach men how to die," to "accept their mortality and, by accepting it, to live through him."[7] We cannot live well if we deny the truth of where we are headed. One day I will know death, up close and personal. This reality must change the way I live as surely as the ocean shapes the shore.

Recalling our death informs the way we live our lives. By accepting our mortality, not denying it, sentimentalizing it, or running from it, we learn to live through Christ. We cease the mad task of living merely to keep ourselves alive. We live knowing that our wealth, strength, and accomplishments are as fleeting as breath itself. We live in view of death so that we might live in light of the hope of new life—knowing that the only way to resurrection is through darkness.

In the *Rule of St. Benedict*, Benedict recommends "Tools for Good Works":

> Day by day remind yourself that you are going to die.
> Hour by hour keep careful watch over all you do,
> aware that God's gaze is upon you, wherever you may be.[8]

Remembering our death doesn't mean we revel in it—we aren't called to a goth celebration of darkness. But reminding ourselves, day by day, that we will die teaches us to live. It allows us to know that the day to seek God, the day to repair relationships, the day to help others and bless the world around us is today—because it may be our last. Meditating on our mortality teaches us to live in light of the larger story of which we are a part, to locate our small joys or tragedies in the scope of eternity.

Ash Wednesday has become central to my experience of time. Each year I need the reality of death proclaimed over me and over my children. I need my church community to remind me of my mortality. I can be tempted to skip too quickly to the resurrection, to skim over the sad stuff, but the liturgical calendar requires me to pause and notice the unresolved chord of our present reality.

At my very first Ash Wednesday service, over a decade ago, I knelt in a quiet sanctuary and was surprised by a feeling of almost irrepressible rage. As the priest marked each forehead with a cross of ashes, I felt like he was marking us for death. I was angry at death. I was angry at the priest as if it was somehow his doing.

I don't want to face the reality of vulnerability—especially the vulnerability of those I love. I'm privileged and healthy enough to maintain the illusion of control. I distract myself from the howling fury of suffering and mortality. I check Facebook. I tweet. I immerse myself in the current political controversy. I get busy. I fill up my life with a thousand other things to avoid noticing the shadow of death.

But I can't shake it. I bump up against it in big and small ways each day. Sleep, sickness, weariness, and nighttime itself are ordinary and unbidden ashes on our foreheads. They say to us: remember that you are going to die. And these daily tokens of mortality are then transformed, by God's mercy, into tools for good works.

When I became a priest, I was suddenly the one marking others with a memento of their death each Lent. In some ways, I love serving as a priest on Ash Wednesday. It is utterly countercultural. Into our shiny, privileged American optimism the ancient church speaks. She forces us to face hard facts. Amid the temptation to a trite denial of mortality, I stand before my church body with an unavoidable truth: "Don't forget," I say, "We are dust. You and I and everyone we know will die. The stuff we live for is fleeting. Hold onto what's real." It's the most punk rock thing I do each year.

But I am not a sadist. Part of me hates being a priest on Ash Wednesday, because the inevitability of death—and more so, the power of capital-D Death and sin—is very bad news. No one goes into ministry to proclaim bad news. We vow our lives to the church because we want to offer hope, we want to extend the good news that we have received about Jesus making the whole world new.

The first time I had to mark a child with a cross of ashes, I wept through the rest of the service. Jonathan can't do it either. He holds it together until he stands over children we know. Our kids or their friends kneel before us with bright expectant faces, so beautiful that a heart can just barely take it. And our job is to mark them with death. He cries through the rest of the service. We're both kind of a mess on Ash Wednesday. I hope we always will be.

I hope it keeps breaking my heart every time I mark someone with a reminder of death because the power of Death is heartbreaking. It's not a fact that we should get used to. It's worth our weeping.

When we pray "bless the dying" we remember those who are at the sharpened point of their own vulnerability. We remember those whose human frailty overwhelms all else and who are—at least temporarily—undone.

But in doing so, we remember that we too are dying. When we ask that God would bless the dying, we ask him to bless us. We watch for the coming kingdom, but we also watch for how God will meet us in this present dying world.

We are dying, each and all. Yet the kind of blessing we most need is the kind that comes to the dying—a blessing we live our life avoiding, a blessing found only in darkness. In the place of deepest desolation, we meet God himself.

10

Soothe the Suffering

Comfort

WHEN MY ELDEST DAUGHTER was learning to read, she would sometimes ask to lead us in Compline. As she said this prayer, she would confidently ask God to "smooth" the suffering, which is what our family prays to this day in her honor.

Categories of human vulnerability—the sick, weary, dying, suffering, afflicted, joyous—are clearly not little boxes that we each fit neatly inside. They blur and shade together. The sick, the dying, the weary, and the afflicted are also "the suffering." Yet we pray for each, one by one. This is not accidental or verbose. Praying for each in turn allows us to pause to honor each kind of human need. We taste different notes in each bitter wine of human misery.

Our common humanity can be found in our shared suffering. We all suffer loss. All of our hearts have been broken. All of us know disappointment. And yet we hold the commonality of our suffering in tension with the reality that hardship is not distributed evenly.

Some have it worse than others. Some of us carry particularly weighty burdens.

It's difficult to discuss suffering generally, since it covers such vast and variegated terrain of human experience. There is physical, emotional, and spiritual suffering—and we each experience these contextually and uniquely. Suffering cannot be painted with a broad brush.

Yet here we are, asking God to soothe the suffering. Or to smooth them, as the case may be.

Scripted prayers—the prayers of Compline, the Psalms, or any other received prayers—are not static. As we pray them, we read our own lives back into the words we pray. Our own biographies shape our understanding of these prayers as much as these prayers shape us and our own stories.

Over years of praying Compline, I have come to think of "the suffering" as those in acute times of pain. There are particular events that divide our lives into before and after. There are seasons of deep darkness, failure, and loss that indelibly mark us.

The year 2017 made me a different person. Before that, I had never lost a parent or a baby. Now I have. For a period of about six months, I was suffering profoundly (and mourning for a long time after that). During that year, nighttime amplified every loneliness and loss; aches echoed and pain roared. Grief was fresh and sharp. Things in my life that had been solid were shaken apart, and the rebuilding had not yet begun.

Here, I am distinguishing between "the suffering" and "the afflicted" because, while periods of suffering do not leave us the same—while they shape the geography of who we are—wounds can lessen with time. Suffering ebbs and flows. It never quite vanishes, but we learn to live again.

The prayer for the afflicted, which comes next in this litany of vulnerability, addresses long-term, chronic suffering. But first, we pray for those in the thick of it, those in intense times of crisis or loss. We pray for those in seasons when the agony and effort of life—of just making it through the day—is pressing and dire, when the darkness seems so vast and terrifying that it threatens to drown all else.

When does one's suffering become enduring and unchanging enough to be counted among "the afflicted?" There's no litmus test. We won't always know whether the suffering we are enduring is temporary or permanent. Not knowing is a part of our vulnerability, and part of what makes suffering scary and difficult. We do not know how long it will last. We do not know when healing will come.

✦ ✦ ✦

"The extreme greatness of Christianity," wrote Simone Weil, "lies in the fact that it does not seek a supernatural remedy for suffering but a supernatural use for it."[1] Christians have always looked to suffering not only as a place of pain, but as a place of meeting God. Suffering does not merely happen *to* us. It works *in* us.

Saint Isaac the Syrian wrote, "The Love of God proceeds from our conversing with Him; this conversation of prayer comes about through stillness, and stillness arrives with the stripping away of self."[2] Notice the order: learning to love God flows from prayer, which flows from stillness, which flows from "the stripping away of the self"—the excruciating relinquishment of our desires and plans.[3]

Suffering strips away the self. This sounds terribly painful, and it is. But the meaning and object of suffering isn't pain; it is to learn to give and receive love. God isn't a sadist who delights in using agony to teach us a lesson. But in the alchemy of redemption, God can take what is only sorrow and transform it into the very path by which we learn to love God and let ourselves be loved. This is the strange (and usually unwanted) way of abundant life—the dying necessary to bring resurrection. Scott Cairns writes, "The hard way is pretty much the only way that most of us manage to learn anything. Affliction, suffering, and pain are—even if they are nothing else—remarkably effective."[4]

There is an entire class of flowers that only bloom at night. Moonflowers, evening primroses, and other night bloomers can only be glimpsed in full glory if you venture out after dark. And there are things in our spiritual lives, too, that only bloom in the dark.

There are things in our spiritual lives, too, that only bloom in the dark.

I'm afraid of the dark, but increasingly I'm more afraid of missing the kind of beauty and growth that can only be found there.

✦ ✦ ✦

Both Paul and Peter tell us that our suffering shares in Christ's own sufferings (Philippians 3:10; 1 Peter 4:13). In suffering we find not only a descent into the depths of anguish, but also—often slowly, and always miraculously—an ascent into Christ's actual life. Not only does Jesus deign to be with us at the graveside of a beloved friend or in triage in the emergency room, but in our suffering we join him in the torment of Gethsemane, the torture of the cross, and the darkness of his own grave.

Paul even says that his own suffering "[fills] up what is lacking in Christ's afflictions" (Colossians 1:24). This has confounded many a theologian (and led to a lot of debate, which helps keep theologians in business). What could it mean? I don't think it means that Jesus didn't quite suffer enough so we need to pony up some misery to clinch our salvation. But it does mean that to find ourselves in Jesus always entails knowing him in pain and suffering. As Augustine puts it, "Jesus' sufferings weren't deficient, but they also continue in and through the church."[5] In Christ, God did not buy us a ticket to a life of ease and non-stop happiness. Instead, we are united to him, so that we grow up into his story through our own stories. The biography of Jesus continues through us, through the church, even through—perhaps especially through—our adversity.

Martin Luther made a distinction between the "theology of the cross" and the "theology of glory." In a theology of glory, God shows his trustworthiness by dolling out pleasure, prosperity, and freedom from suffering to the righteous. In contrast, the theology of the cross discovers God "hidden in suffering."[6] A theology of glory has the same logic as any empire: that power, money, and pleasure are the stuff of greatness. The theology of the cross teaches that the kingdom of God is topsy-turvy—that God is most present in the darkest moments of our lives.

We are tempted to see wellness, wealth, and success as evidence of God's favor, and suffering as the place of God's absence or a punishment for sin. If, when we face pain and disappointment, we wonder whether God is actually looking out for us, we have imbibed the theology of glory. We are seeking a God who will keep bad things from happening to us.

To love God through suffering means learning that when we look for evidence of God's work in our lives, it is often in the last place we'd want to find it: in weakness, in pain, in the cross.

So do we have to be impassive or even upbeat when enduring a cross? No. Jesus himself showed no sign of placidity on the cross. He wept, he lamented, he cried out to God in anguish, he admitted his need, his pain, his thirst. We need not paper over our pain, or anyone else's. We weep.

But even as we weep, we watch for the One the Scriptures call "the God of all comfort."

✦ ✦ ✦

God himself is the Comforter. It is one of the meanings of *parakletos*, the name Jesus gives to the Holy Spirit, literally the one "called alongside" us to help. We share in the sufferings of Christ with the promise that "through Christ we share abundantly in comfort too" (2 Corinthians 1:3-7).

In the first few verses of Paul's second letter to the Corinthians, the words *comfort* and *suffering* positively dance.

C. FitzSimons Allison says that what is on display here is the "essential connection" between the Holy Spirit and both Christ's and our suffering. Paul—never one to mind repetition—mentions comfort ten times and suffering seven times in just a few short sentences. Allison sums up these verses by saying that while the desire to escape suffering is understandable, to do so leaves us "bereft of true life, peace, fellowship, endurance, character, hope, and, most of all, God's Comforter."[7] To walk with God in suffering is to know sorrow, confusion, frustration, and doubt, but also, in time, to find the comfort our souls most long for and cannot find anywhere else.

In the end, we find comfort only in the presence of the Comforter.

But it is a strange kind of comfort. It is hard-won. It's not the comfort of high thread-count sheets and chocolate truffles, or a good cup of tea and a warm blanket, though these are certainly gifts from God. The comfort we find in suffering is not the stuff of luxury or coziness.

What's on offer is what Saint Isaac the Syrian called "vision of soul." Suffering gives us new eyes; it teaches us to see in the dark. And what do we learn to see? Light, hope, joy, even God himself, in new and profound ways.

In our suffering we can receive this gift of "vision of soul," but doing so is not compulsory. We are just as free to curse God for our suffering as seek him in it. But if we are to discover the things that only bloom in the dark, if we are to meet any glory in our own crosses, we must cooperate with the work that suffering does in us.

It's a seemingly insane calling: to cooperate with God in our own undoing.

The crosses we are called to carry are never things we'd choose. Yet Christian practices of prayer help us receive the growth that comes in ways we least want. Suffering—the "stripping away of the self"—is not inherently good or valuable.

It is useless unless it gives way to stillness, then prayer, and ultimately to the love of God.

In M. C. Escher's famous lithograph, a hand is drawing another hand, which itself is bent back drawing the hand that is drawing it—a circle of hands drawing each other. In suffering there is another mysterious circle: We pray to endure the mystery of suffering, and the mystery of suffering teaches us to pray. And the end of all of it is the love of God. That's what we discover in the center of the circle.

Comfort in pain is a human need. We need soothing as surely as we need food and water. So if we do not find solace in God the Comforter, we will inevitably seek it elsewhere, and what we habitually go to for comfort is eventually what we worship. It becomes our god. But when these other comforts, however good in themselves, become our soul's refuge, they tend to kill us.

The song "Creature Comfort" by Arcade Fire is about "the white lie of American prosperity." It's a song about self-harm and suicide, boys who "hate themselves" and girls who "hate their bodies." These suffering ones pray a haunting prayer throughout the song:

> God, make me famous
> If You can't, just make it painless
> Just make it painless.[8]

Make me famous or make it painless. Either way, take away the awful feelings of weakness and wounding.

In times when sorrow is so deep that I can feel it in my body, I go almost instinctually to anything that I can use as morphine: the internet, television, carbs, exercise, sleep, staying up late, wine, chocolate, work, social media.

Dennis Byrne writes in the *Chicago Tribune*, "Time to face it: We are a nation of addicts." He says that around 40 million

Americans are addicted to drugs or alcohol—merely two of the myriad of things to which we go to soothe the pain. Byrne says that our society embraces "so many addictions it's hard to list them all." Not just your standard sex, pornography, tobacco, and alcohol, but also food, video games, the internet, sweets, work, retweets, and so much more. He asks, "What are we running from that we're so compelled to search for, create and overdose on so many props?"[9]

In his book *The Elephant in the Room*, Tommy Tomlinson explores his addiction to food. He speaks for all of us with our various addictions: "This is the cruel trick of most addictions. They're so good at short term comfort. I'm hungry, I'm lonely, I need to feel a part of the world. Other people soothe those pains with the bottle or the needle. I soothe them with burgers and fries. It pushes the hurt down the road a little bit."[10] When we are suffering, we need soothing, and when we have no idea where to find it, we learn to kick the pain a little further down the road.

The suffering need soothing, not just numbing. We need real hope, the kind that can carry us through the night.

Certainly God comforts us through the good stuff of earth, the smell of coffee or the sound of rain on a tin roof. But when the drifts of suffering pile deeper and higher, it becomes clear that creature comforts will ultimately never be enough. Even good gifts diminish us when we turn to them compulsively in our pain.

God, on the other hand, does not make our lives painless. But God is a true Comforter.

To walk through suffering as a Christian—to share in Christ's sufferings—we have to face the darkness. We have to feel the things we hate to feel—sadness, loss, loneliness. We have to drink the bitter cup we've been given. No shortcuts. No free passes. But this is the strange way of true comfort. It's the only way to discover soothing that is substantial enough to bear the weight of our souls.

Everything in us wants to numb the pain. So in this prayer we ask for soothing—for ourselves and for others—because if we go to pleasure or distraction like anesthesia, we lose the enduring comfort that can only be received in vulnerability. Soothing of suffering comes, always and only, as a gift.

✦ ✦ ✦

Christian asceticism has gotten a bad rap lately. Any denial of pleasure is associated with the worst kind of puritanical legalism. While cleanses and fad diets are all the rage, self-denial for spiritual formation is suspect. Celibacy, chastity, and abstinence are dismissed as absurd, if not destructive, associated with body-shaming and opposed to "sex positivity." Fasting is overzealous and fanatical. Faith, we assume, should never make us feel bad, so asceticism is considered useless, legalistic, or inhumane.

I must admit outright: I'm the least of ascetics. By the standards of almost anyone in the ancient church, I'm a hedonist. I'm not particularly proud of this. Yet, when it comes to chocolate or sleeping late or media consumption, I have about as much self-restraint as a drunk hamster. I'm terrible at fasting. Lent for me is usually an adventure in failure. Twice I've given up Lent for Lent, in what can only be described as a complete cop-out. If you need a priest to pontificate about the glory of God in the stuff of creation, the pleasures that lead us to wonder and worship, the spiritual goodness that can be found in ice cream or a lazy Saturday or a long nap, I'm your girl. I've penned treatises on the eternal value of pleasure and beauty, and I absolutely stand by them. And yet Christian austerity—a temporary embrace of suffering for a greater love—is also enormously significant in the witness of the church and the practice of Christian spirituality.

There is no contradiction here. Christian asceticism is never meant to be a denial of the goodness of materiality or embodiment. Christianity is an earthy, pleasure-affirming faith.

But Christians have often practiced self-denial in order to learn to enjoy good things in their proper place.

We embrace ascetic practices to learn to suffer. We know that we all inevitably will suffer, so we practice it ahead of time. It's an exercise in discomfort. We train our need for comfort like people housetrain puppies. By doing so, we learn over time how to enter into a soothing that is deeper than what's offered by our drug of choice. We learn to face the pain we are avoiding. Christian asceticism is a bit like homoeopathy— exposing us to a tiny dose of suffering to bring healing in the larger areas of loss, sin, and spiritual sickness in our lives.

> *Christian asceticism is a bit like homoeopathy— exposing us to a tiny dose of suffering to bring healing in the larger areas of loss, sin, and spiritual sickness in our lives.*

Ascetic practices reveal the way we use creature comforts, however good in themselves, compulsively. We deny ourselves some small pleasure, some perceived need, and we find what slaves we have become to the things we use to console ourselves.

I'm not suggesting that periods of profound suffering are the right times to practice self-denial. In these seasons, just getting through the day alive can feel like an ascetic experience. (And if in the depths of pain, all you can do to keep going is sit before God and eat some ice cream or smoke a pipe or watch a movie with greasy fries—for the literal love of God, do so.)

But our cultural resistance to any kind of "stripping away of the self" leaves us unprepared for the suffering and trauma that life inevitably deals out to all of us. Even we Christians have often never been taught a spirituality thick enough to sustain us when all other comforts run dry. Since birth we have been nurtured on the logic of consumerism—that pain can be erased, or at least dulled through enough consumption. If we can buy enough, be successful enough, be famous enough, imbibe enough, get the girl or the guy, get the home and the career, then our suffering can be soothed. We can even use spirituality in the same way, marketing God or the spiritual life as the path of self-fulfillment and triumph, not the way of a cross. We've been brought up on this lie like a daily vitamin, and it has harmed us—as people, as a culture, as a church.

In his piece "I Used to Be a Human Being," Andrew Sullivan, a journalist who had been a popular blogger, discusses how he quit what he calls his "addiction" to technology and social media. He wanted to learn to practice silence. He went on a retreat that required silence all day and night, with no cell phone, internet, GPS, or even conversation.

A few days into his retreat he was suddenly—to his surprise—overwhelmed by painful childhood memories, in particular the suffering he endured due to his mother's mental illness. He wrote, "It was as if, having slowly and progressively removed every distraction from my life, I was suddenly faced with what I had been distracting myself from. Resting for a moment against the trunk of a tree, I stopped, and suddenly found myself bent over, convulsed with the newly present pain, sobbing." Every crutch he had habitually turned to had been taken away. He couldn't call or text a friend; he couldn't check Twitter or email. He had to sit in the pain of his long-buried childhood trauma. And what he found was that he not only survived the experience, but that he found healing through it.

There is wisdom that can be wrought only in self-denial—only when all our other props, devices, and numbing agents are taken away. Sullivan writes, "The sadness shifted into a kind of calm and rest. I felt other things from my childhood—the beauty of the forests, the joy of friends, the support of my sister, the love of my maternal grandmother."[11] He spent a lifetime avoiding suffering, but the only way to the other side was through it. The only way he could find healing was by denying himself the thing that gave him an identity and a career, the thing he most compulsively went to for comfort.

Christian asceticism, the practice of silence, fasting, chastity, celibacy, solitude, or some other form of self-denial, is not for self-destruction or self-condemnation but for healing. As we take up suffering in big and small ways, we learn to seek soothing in ways that are not particularly natural to us, but are deeply needed. We train our hearts to seek enduring comfort in God himself. We practice ridding ourselves of our gloriously good but inadequate creature comforts in order to learn to receive the solace for which we most deeply long.

✦ ✦ ✦

We ask God to "soothe the suffering." We don't ask him to placate the suffering with clichés. We don't ask that the sufferer would quiet down and get over it. We look to God as a gentle nurturer, a comforter, and healer, not as a gruff coach who tells us to stop whining and play through the pain.

A woman in my congregation was about ten months into the hard work of grieving the death of her husband when I heard through the grapevine that someone had told her that she'd been sad long enough; it was time to buck up and get over it.

This is not soothing the suffering, but rushing them.

When I heard about this, what kicked in was a kind of maternal impulse to protect the suffering member of my congregation. I felt wrathful, and a bit self-righteous about it. But then I began to recall the times when I myself am impatient with the suffering. I can set up my own subconscious timetables, for myself or others, about how long suffering should last. But most often, healing takes longer than we think it should. The quick fix is always a temptation, but the quick fix for the suffering is dishonesty, addiction, and the denial of their humanity. Even in the church we often want people to help themselves, fix themselves, and save themselves—and hurry it up already.

But as we learn to long for God to soothe us and others, we also learn to wait on the slow process of him doing so.

Does God ever bring emotional or spiritual or even physical healing in an instant? Sometimes. He certainly can. But soothing most often looks like tiny provisions, crags of grace on a long climb. There is healing in the Christian life. There is soothing. I've tasted it and seen it, but we don't get to choose when or how it comes.

Pierre Teilhard de Chardin reminds us, "Above all, trust in the slow work of God." We ask the Lord to soothe the suffering, and then we remember de Chardin's call:

Give Our Lord the benefit of believing
that his hand is leading you,
and accept the anxiety of feeling yourself
in suspense and incomplete.[12]

✦ ✦ ✦

There's the old saying, "What doesn't kill you makes you stronger." But this rings hollow to me, and I suspect to most anyone who has suffered.

The condition that eventually killed my father suddenly first began as a slow process of decline. During a long stretch of hospital stays, I spent days holding his hand. Then my daughters both got a stomach bug, and I spent nights holding back their hair as they vomited. In the midst of those exhausting weeks I wrote, "I do not feel that these hard days, these stresses and sorrows and challenges, make me stronger. In the end . . . I feel profoundly weak and vulnerable."

It was Nietzsche who first said the now-famous cliché about "what does not kill us." It's from his book, *Twilight of the Idols*: "Out of Life's School of War: what does not kill me makes me stronger."[13]

I face things every day, big and small, that are difficult but have not killed me. And I'm finding that what doesn't kill me actually makes me weaker, and maybe that's the point—that the way of glory is discovered through, and only through, the cross. In life's school of love, suffering—what doesn't kill us— makes us more alive to our need and helplessness and, therefore, more able to give and receive love.

Certainly suffering builds resilience, just as a broken bone heals stronger. We can be, perhaps ironically, more fragile if we never know pain or struggle. And there is a kind of hardy faith- fulness and grit to be found on the far side of agony. But this kind of resilience does not form us into Nietzsche's vision of impenetrable toughness; it does not harden us. It makes us more open to our belovedness in God, to our own vulnerability, and to the vulnerability of others.

In her essay "The Tabernacling of God and a Theology of Weakness," Marva Dawn says that

> even as Christ accomplished atonement for us by suffering and death, so the Lord accomplishes witness to the world through our weakness. . . . God's way is not to take us out of tribulations, but to comfort us in the midst of them and "exchange" our strength in the face of them. By our union with Christ in the power of the Spirit in our weaknesses, we display God's glory.[14]

The people who I most respect are those who have suffered but did not numb their pain—who faced their darkness. In the process they have become beautifully weak, not tough as nails, not bitter or rigid, but men and women who bear vulnerability with joy and trust. They are almost luminescent, like a paper lantern, weak enough that light shines through.

Pity the Afflicted

Relentlessness and Revelation

IF "THE SUFFERING" ARE THOSE in seasons of deep pain, "the afflicted" are those who walk through prolonged, even lifelong anguish.[1] These are the ones whose bodies will never work well this side of the grave, who suffer loneliness that will not abate, who bear particularly weighty burdens and trauma, or who have fewer nets to catch them when they fall.

And for the afflicted, nighttime can be particularly grueling.

Dementia patients, for instance, face a phenomenon known as "sundowning." For reasons doctors don't completely understand, confusion, anxiety, and aggression get worse around the time the sun sets. Those with chronic depression or anxiety also see their symptoms worsen at night.[2]

I used to work with teenagers who lived on the streets. The pressing danger that these kids, especially the young women, faced at night was almost unimaginable. The majority had been sexually assaulted on the streets, under the cover of darkness, often multiple times.

My friends Steven and Bethany lead street retreats.[3] They take people on spiritual retreats, but instead of withdrawing to a monastery or the mountains, they spend time among the homeless on the sidewalks and alleyways of Austin, Texas. The point of these retreats is not to simulate poverty or give privileged people a taste of homelessness—obviously spending a night or two on the streets is nothing like being homeless. The point, in Steven's words, is to "seek Jesus where he promises to be found," among the poor and the needy—among the afflicted. For a couple nights, participants experience the vulnerability of sleeping outside in the city at night. But on those dark streets, among the afflicted, people meet God. Steven says that even those who don't call themselves believers tell of experiences in which "they met the sublime."

Steven and Bethany have a lot of friends on the streets, and the afflicted extend hospitality to them. They are welcomed into homeless camps and given advice about where to sleep most comfortably. When they brought their five-month-old on a retreat with them, someone showed them the safest places to spend the night with their baby. One friend they met on the street prayed for them, asking for angels to protect them, for their safety in the night, and that they'd meet the morning with a good breakfast. Bethany tells me, "Affliction and grace travel together."

Unearned gifts of health, youth, education, financial security, family, and community shield me from the full force of the broken world. My life, however imperfect, has a level of stability and safety that's unimaginable for most people on earth.

I have experienced suffering, but I still don't know the true depths of human affliction. To witness loved ones—even strangers—whose lives are full of hardship or torment leaves me reeling. How do we find the goodness of God in the midst of affliction? Does the very existence of such agonizing lives preclude our trust in a kind God? What hope is there for whole

> *Does the very existence of such agonizing lives preclude our trust in a kind God?*

communities of people whose suffering goes on unabated? For the child whose seizures will only worsen until she dies? For the girls who cannot remember life before they were trafficked for sex? For the mentally ill who have lived decades in institutions or on the street?

In this prayer we ask God to "pity the afflicted." The word *pity* has fallen on hard times. It seems woefully inadequate for what we long for. It sometimes invokes defensiveness, as in, "I don't need your pity." But the root of the word *pity* is from the Old French word for compassion. To feel pity is to share in someone else's sadness, to commiserate with another's suffering. In a world prone to tribalism and outrage, to hardheartedness, judgment, and apathy, we all need as much pity as we can get, both from God and others.

And here again, this prayer challenges my assumptions. We don't ask God directly to take away the affliction of the afflicted—though he might, out of pity. That's what I most want to ask: "Dear God, end all affliction."

And our hope is that God will. Someday.

But for now, we ask that God would show sympathy. In this particular prayer, we don't ask for a permanent solution, but for God to suffer with us, which is what compassion literally means. We ask that God might feel what we feel, to enter into the dark room in which we find ourselves and sit with us in our pain and vulnerability. It's a bold ask: that God himself would suffer with the alcoholic, the homeless kid, the Alzheimer's patient, the bipolar woman in a manic spell—that somehow the Holy One would feel precisely and palpably what they are feeling. We're asking that God see this kind of pain and enter into its depths, not as a voyeur but as one who suffers with us.

✦ ✦ ✦

Christians believe that God himself walks with the afflicted, and that we are called to do the same.

This can be a difficult vocation. Early on in my job as a parish priest it became clear to me that my church often did a great job of walking with those in crisis. If someone was in the hospital, if someone had surgery, lost a job, or had a family member die, we showed up with casseroles and prayers and tears and help. It was beautiful to watch. What's harder for us, though, is walking with those in long-term need.

You need five meals after a hip replacement? We've got you. You need three meals a week for the next ten years? We have no idea how to make that happen. You need a pastoral visit every week or two for the rest of your life? That's probably more than we can do. We have social workers in our congregation we call when we encounter longer, ongoing needs, but most churches aren't set up as a social work agency. We are, after all, mostly reliant on volunteers and there's usually a handful of people in acute crisis at any given time.

But this also hints at a deeper struggle in the broader church, at least here in the United States, that makes it hard for us to suffer with the afflicted. We often don't know how to walk with people when the road is long and there will likely be no happy ending.

During my own crisis in 2017, I was talking to a friend who's a national ministry leader. He's observed and studied the American church for years, and almost offhandedly he said, "We all kind of believe the prosperity gospel, don't we? We expect God to make our life work out. And that if we do our part, he has to make things go well for us."[4] To be sure, most Christians both worldwide and in the United States would admit that the prosperity gospel—the idea that God rewards the righteous with health and wealth—is not true. This is not Christian theology. It's a modern day version of the "theology of glory" that Luther condemned. And yet, in some silent place in our hearts, we sense God's pleasure when things go well for us and his disapproval—if not outright absence—in our disappointments. This births a species of Christian faith that wants resolution, performance, and results, and we often have a hard time knowing how to face and help others face situations where suffering will not resolve any time soon, where the burdens people carry will not be lifted. We want suffering to have a clear beginning, middle, and end, something we can get through, a story with a tidy resolution. We buck against a vision of Christianity with no immediate results, no clear payoff.

The lives of the afflicted remind us, uncomfortably, that suffering is not simply a problem to be solved.

I have a friend whose son has severe autism. My friend often wonders what to pray for his son. Despite all the struggles of parenting that the rest of us go through—potty training and managing conflict, illness and injury—we imagine that someday our kids will be independent and need us less. But my friend's son will depend on his parents as long as they live. They will likely never hear him tell about his day, or teach him how to tie his shoes. My friend loves his son, deeply and desperately, and because of this very love he suffers deeply, and there's no end in sight to this suffering. He bears the weight of his son's affliction.

Of course, that's not the whole story. My friend finds delight and joy in his son as well. He tells stories about his son with beaming pride and laughter. His son serves their local church and blesses the people around him. But grief is also ever-present, swelling with every milestone his son will likely never meet, every normal rite of passage that he will not know. What is the hope for my friend and for his son? What does prayer for him look like? What does the "abundant life" in Jesus look like for those whose lives will never look anything like the American dream?

✦ ✦ ✦

What further complicates the thorny subject of affliction and God's goodness is that we not only serve a God who does not remove all affliction, sometimes he seems to send us into it headlong. Often it's our convictions, borne from the ethical rigor of the Christian faith, that lead us away from the path of ease and happiness. I have friends who have continued their pregnancies, keeping their children with disabilities even when doctors told them to abort. I have friends who give away most of their income, taking on burdens of budgeting that they could easily avoid if they were less generous. I have friends who remain in unhappy marriages, who seek help from counselors year after year, and yet endure. And I have friends who remain single and celibate because of their convictions.

Persecuted Christians all over the world face a choice between apostasy and death, and thousands upon thousands choose death. There are international students in my own church whose conversion to Christianity means they are cut off from home or family. With their baptism, they trade a well-paved road to happiness and wealth in their home country for a life fleeing persecution.

As Western Christians we can find it hard to believe that God would call us to embrace any kind of pain that will not soon resolve. We recoil from a God who would allow affliction, or whose ethical standards would ever spur on affliction. In *God in the Dock*, C. S. Lewis famously said, "I didn't go to religion to make me happy. I always knew a bottle of Port would do that. If you want a religion to make you feel really comfortable, I certainly don't recommend Christianity." Instead he recommends self-worship, which he says will make you pretty happy in the short term, or he says, some "patent American article on the market" would do as well—a spirituality that promises that everything we want is probably what God wants for us too.[5]

The truth of Christianity leads to human flourishing. But it is always a flourishing that, to quote Aquinas, is an "arduous good."[6] Ron Belgau, a committed celibate, writes, "An arduous good is a good that requires struggle. A good that is worth fighting for. And a good that inspires fear and hope and endurance in the face of adversity. 'Arduous good' is also a phrase that is seldom spoken in Hollywood, and almost never heard on Madison Avenue." And, I'd add, it's rarely heard in the church as well. But, Belgau writes, salvation itself is "an arduous good, a treasure buried in a field, the pearl of great price, for which we will gladly sacrifice everything."[7]

That the Christian faith motivates suffering is not a hidden dimension of the faith, something we keep under wraps promising an ever exciting and glorious life instead. It's not a bait and switch. Jesus calls people to a cross—to die, to lose their life so that they might gain it. He was positively terrible at PR. He was not a salesman. But, on the other hand, he drank his own poison. He was honest about the cost of discipleship and about pain that is not easily solved. He embraced all of it with pity, and with his own body.

I don't know why God allows affliction, but I do know this: he is found among the afflicted.

Through my work, I've heard from many people whose life in Christ is shaped by affliction—their own affliction or the affliction of those they love. I met one man who spent much of his day caring for his mother who had advanced dementia. He told me that he had never considered that helping his mom was a formative spiritual practice in his life. Discovering that it could be had changed him.

I was amazed. How could he not have seen something so profoundly self-emptying, so gloriously near to the compassion of God, as a spiritual practice? He told me, "Because I'd never have chosen it."

We think of spiritual practices as things we take up, like reading the Scriptures, prayer, or church attendance. These are the straightforwardly spiritual parts of our days. The rest of life is just what we get through, the inert stuff of time, chance, and biography. But often the most foundational and shaping spiritual practices of our lives are things we'd never have chosen. The most profound ways that we encounter God are often in affliction.

In his book *Strong and Weak*, Andy Crouch writes about his niece Angela who was born with a genetic condition, Trisomy 13. Beating all the odds, she was still alive at age eleven, but couldn't see, hear, or walk. Crouch writes, "She could not feed or bathe herself; she knew nothing of language. We could only guess what she knew of her mother, father, grandparents, brother and sisters." Is this flourishing? Crouch admits that Angela cannot flourish by "any definition held out to us by mass-affluent consumer culture." And yet, he says, because of Angela's life, even in affliction, those around her know greater flourishing. He writes, "The real test of every human community is how it cares for the most vulnerable, those like Angela who cannot sustain even a simulation of independence and autonomy."[8] Because of Angela's great vulnerability, her doctors, family, and friends are able to act for her good, and this creates community flourishing for those around her in ways that they would not have otherwise known.

Mother Teresa said that the afflicted are Christ in his most "distressing disguise."[9] He shows pity on the afflicted, and through them, on us. He exposes the empty promise of a consumer culture, and indeed a consumer faith—that ease, prosperity, health, and present fulfillment are true abundance. The afflicted unmask the lie that what makes life worth living

> *Often the most foundational and shaping spiritual practices of our lives are things we'd never have chosen.*

and God worth knowing are the pleasures I can wrench from my days.

Life is full of affliction, and the way of Jesus is arduous. He never promised differently. What he promises is abundant life, and it takes a lifetime of practicing this craft of the Christian faith to gain an idea of what that looks like. But the afflicted teach me that it isn't what I think it is; it isn't a perfect marriage or a life of endless success. It is always a cross and a resurrection.

✦ ✦ ✦

If we hold up the mere existence of the afflicted as proof of God's distance, the afflicted themselves often tell of his nearness. I am regularly astonished that those in affliction frequently trust God in ways that the rest of us find difficult.

In his book *Enduring Divine Absence*, the philosopher Joseph Minich discusses how skepticism grows amid wealth, comfort, and privilege. The rejection of belief in God is most often, he says, "a white, well-to-do phenomenon."[10]

Comedian Neal Brennan jokes, "It's funny, I know a lot of white atheists, but I don't know a lot of black ones, and I got a theory about why: Because atheism is really the height of white privilege. . . . Think about it: Religion basically says, 'Hey, can we interest you in an after-life?' And white people are all like, 'No, thank you.' Like, 'Why? How much better can it be?'"[11]

Among the poor, both here in the United States and even more so in developing nations, belief blossoms—and not the glossy, permissive spirituality trendy among urbane Westerners, but belief of the more traditional, orthodox variety. At the beginning of the twentieth century, 80 percent of all Christians were in Europe and North America, with only 20 percent in the non-Western world. Now it's almost the reverse—two-thirds of the world's Christians live in the Global South. This is due not so much to the decline of faith in the West but to the explosive growth of the church in the rest of the world.[12]

I see this in my own Anglican Communion, where Christian faith wanes in wealthy Western nations and blossoms in the Global South. Of course, not all the Anglicans in Africa, Latin America, and Asia are poor or afflicted, but many endure hardship, poverty, and religious persecution that I cannot imagine. And yet they trust God in ways that leave me dumbfounded.

Take, for example, Archbishop Benjamin Kwashi. In 2008 he became the Anglican Archbishop of Jos, a region on the contested border that divides northern Islamic Nigeria from the southern predominately Christian Nigeria. Over the course of his ministry, he has seen hundreds of churches bombed. His own home was bombed. His wife was beaten and raped by terrorists, and he has nearly been murdered on several occasions. In the midst of this persecution, Archbishop Kwashi was able to say, "If God spares my life, no matter how short or long that is, I have something worth living and dying for. So I'm going to do that quickly and urgently. That kind of faith is what I am passing on to the coming generations. This world is not our home, we are strangers here, we've got business to do, so let's get on and do it."[13]

Though statistics show that here in the West young people in particular drift into unbelief partly because of the problem of evil, it seems that our prosperity renders far more doubt than the afflicted find in their affliction.

A common explanation of this is that the afflicted need the crutch of cosmic comfort, whereas the heathy and wealthy, with our advanced medicine, working water heaters, and craft beer, have no need of such an aid.

But I'd contend that all of us—every last man, woman, and child —walk with crutches. We all need help. We need something to bear our weight. In our truest and most naked state, we are all deeply vulnerable.

The afflicted reveal to us our true state. We meet Jesus in his "distressing disguise," and in him we see true humanity. All that we rely on to make our lives work, from the electric grid to our own minds, can be lost. All our purported strength and autonomy are flimsy. If the most vulnerable among us need God as a crutch to bear the weight of their lives, perhaps they're just more honest about what we all need. Hardship can breed humility, which allows us to see God more clearly because we become more honest about who we truly are. Maybe spiritual hunger—that we suppress but never satisfy by money, privilege, and health—is not born of naiveté, but of reality.

We are all in constant need of sustenance. We are all in need of God's pity.

✦ ✦ ✦

A few years ago I encountered a horrendously unjust situation overseas. Children were used as bait to bring in money from American adoptive parents, but those running their orphanage made no effort to go through legal processes that would allow these kids to move into permanent homes. So these kids were stuck. They were captives, used for profit, and perpetually kept from families who desperately wanted them. It was illegal, but law enforcement was bribed. Nothing would be done for these children, the poorest of the poor, orphaned in a remote part of East Africa.

I was a new mother when I found out about this situation and I could not look at my own child without seeing the faces of these children. I burned with maternal rage. There was nothing I could do to rescue these kids, and it seemed there would be no justice. The situation was helpless. The only comfort I could find was that God saw what was happening, and that he is the judge of injustice.

I rarely resonate with the image of Jesus as a judge. I gravitate to my hippie version of Jesus, with a flower tucked behind his ear. I'm drawn to his grace, his kindness, his beauty. But when I encounter those afflicted by entrenched injustice, I yearn for a God who sees, and who will work on behalf of those abandoned by the world.

Ultimately our hope is not only that Christ will be found among the afflicted, but that affliction itself will end. We hope—and pray—that God's pity is active, that God works decisively to restore the afflicted and to judge, defeat, and destroy every cause of affliction.

When we encounter affliction, we long for a day when everything that is broken—in our bodies, in nature, in relationships, in society, in politics, in policing, in global economics—will be mended and made right. We yearn for an "end" to affliction in both senses of the word—that there is a telos, a design, to all this seemingly needless and random human suffering, but also that affliction will be overcome and abolished. This is our hope: that heaven will crash into earth, that all that is now hidden will be revealed before the judgment and mercy of Jesus, that he will judge all those who take advantage of the weak and every dark force that brings despair and pain into the world. This is the vision of the future that grounds our thirst for justice here and now.

The shape of our prayers determines the shape of our life. Praying each night for those whose suffering will not abate shapes our mission in the world.

The shape of our prayers determines the shape of our life.

We cannot ask God to pity the afflicted—to suffer with them and redeem their affliction—without also joining God in that work of pity. We work to care for the afflicted, to affirm the dignity of every human being as an image bearer of God. We advocate for systems and laws that support justice and flourishing for the weakest and most defenseless. We ask God to pity the afflicted and, consequently, we use our own money, health, time, education, and privilege to bless them too, whether they live a continent away or in our own living rooms.

As a church, we seek to be a people of active compassion toward the afflicted, knowing that God identifies with them in their affliction. We will not set everything right—not nearly. Not all suffering will end. We will not bring heaven to earth. But we can and must push back against the darkness, even as we await the dawn.

12

Shield the Joyous

Gratitude and Indifference

A FEW MONTHS INTO writing this book, Jonathan and I found, to our great surprise, that I was pregnant. We'd had two children, then lost two children to miscarriage. Two years later, here we were again. Pregnant. At forty. I was thrilled and terrified, and terrified of feeling thrilled.

In this fallen world, joy is risky.

Joy takes courage. Vulnerability is plainly on display in suffering and grief, but we also taste it simply by knowing that we live in a fallen world where we can never see around the bend.

So I trick myself into believing that if I don't take up joy or celebration, that maybe, just maybe, it won't hurt so much when grief rises like the tide. I hedge my bets, wait for the other shoe to drop, and protect myself from pain by avoiding the wonder and beauty before me. I try to shield myself from disappointment by not embracing joy.

In this prayer we recognize the vulnerability of joy. We ask God to shield the joyous, to protect that part of us that's courageous enough to believe that good things happen.

Because good things do happen. A baffling part about walking with a God who does not keep bad things from happening is that it's clear that he makes good things happen also—and often. God is maddeningly unpredictable and free.

Each day of our lives holds relentless beauty, mercy, grace upon grace. Babies are born healthy every day. Marriages recover from the depths of contempt. Many—not all—of us awake each day with bodies that work. We can do good work, brew tea, take a walk, breathe autumn air, and crunch leaves beneath our feet. We laugh. We dance. We heal. Cancer goes into remission. People recover from illness. Mangos grow. Dead coral reefs slowly regenerate. These things happen, and they happen by grace. They are gifts from God that we are called to receive with open hands.

We have to learn to trust God in order to receive even good things from him. And learning to receive good things from God is difficult, especially if you've been hurt. It's hard to learn to trust goodness and beauty. It takes practice to face the reality of darkness, but also to ask for—and hope for—light.

To risk joy requires hope. And hope is the opposite of anxiety. I am habitually anxious. I catastrophize. I plan for the worst. This habit leads me to, as they say in the South, "borrow trouble." Horrors could happen, so I start mourning them ahead of time—it's never too early to get a jump start on misery.

To hope is to "borrow grace." It is not naive optimism. Hope admits the truth of our vulnerability. It does not trust God to keep all bad things from happening. But it assumes that redemption, beauty, and goodness will be there for us, whatever lies ahead.

When we found out we were pregnant again, we sat our two daughters down to tell them. Our youngest daughter responded by jumping up and down, spinning around in glee, and kissing my swollen belly. Our older daughter burst into tears and laid her head in her father's lap, wailing, "The baby is going to die again!" She still remembered the feeling of getting our collective breath knocked out of us by heartbreak. She remembered the burial service we had for her unborn brother. This new announcement, however joyous, resurfaced old pain and trauma. Love always involves risk, and loving again means risking again.[1]

In their dual responses to our news, my two daughters embodied the war in my own soul. I was hopeful and excited. I wanted to embrace the joy of this good news. But being pregnant opened me up to potential heartbreak. We could not promise our daughters that this baby would not die. We had no idea if our celebrating would turn to mourning or if our mourning would turn to celebrating. We had to wait in the unknowing, and allow hope to slowly unfurl without any guarantees about how this story would end.

That night our older daughter, a burgeoning artist, spent hours drawing half a dozen pictures with the same theme: her new brother. She drew pictures of our family with a baby, of herself as a teenager with a little brother, of her brother learning to walk. This was her way to reach for hope. She was praying in pencil and crayon. She took the brave step of allowing herself to feel excitement again, and in doing so, she opened herself to the possibility of pain. She was risking the vulnerability of joy, trusting God that it wasn't a bad risk—not because we could count on any outcome, but because we could count on God to shield us.

I have to learn again and again to risk joy, to intentionally practice hope. A friend gave me some baby booties that she knit for our son. Tiny, adorable leather-soled boots in green and brown. I decided to put them on our mantle, where I left them for months, waiting for our son. This was my exercise in joy, letting them sit in that honored place as a token of hope. But it was also like laying them on an altar, waiting to receive whatever God would bring.

✦ ✦ ✦

A slow, cold river cuts through the land behind my late grand-parents' (now my mother's) home. It is my favorite place. It's in Central Texas and even in years when drought scorches the land and kills the crops, the river continues to flow. Its source is a deep subterranean aquifer, where some two hundred springs blast from fissures in the rock deep below the surface. Those springs have been there since the dawn of time, and I suspect that river will continue as long as the earth itself.

This is my picture of joy—this place of beauty, this steadfast presence. I dip my hand in the rippling water, but what I can touch is only the surface of deep unfailing currents.

Christians have what theologians call a sacramental view of reality.[2] We believe that the stuff of earth carries within it the sacred presence of God. When we find bliss, wonder, or glory, we brush up against a solid reality: God's own truth, beauty, and goodness. We delight in these things because they participate in God.

After a meditation on frailty and loss, this prayer recalls the breathtaking loveliness and levity that remain in the world despite the heartache.

Just as this prayer reminds us that each night there are people who are sick or dying or suffering or afflicted, it also brings to mind those whose night sparkles with beauty, hope, and joy. Somewhere there is a young couple spending their first evening together as husband and wife. There are travelers seeing the northern lights. There are people clinking champagne glasses. There are families curled up happily in pajamas watching their favorite movie. There are friends gathered around a meal, trading stories, drunk with talk, not wanting the night to end.

These moments are sacramental. They participate in a reality that is sacred and sturdy.

And yet we know these good gifts can be lost—and one day, when we die, all will be lost for a little while.

Yet we believe that joy will remain. Joy must therefore be more than simply happiness.

The apostles sound a little crazy when they talk about joy. James goes so far as to say that when we face trials we ought to "count it all joy" (James 1:2). The only way this could make any sense is if joy is anchored in bedrock. In deepest anguish, when bliss is nowhere to be found, the truth, goodness, and beauty that we met in our happiest moments does not cease to be real or reliable. When good gifts are lost, the Giver remains—and the Giver is the ultimate source of joy to begin with, the reality to which sacramental reality points.

So Christians unapologetically embrace that good, earthy gifts bring joy, even as we also proclaim an enduring joy that remains even when all pleasures are burned away. To practice joy then is to seek the source of all that is lovely and bright.

A nine-year-old at my church was asked by his mom what this prayer to "shield the joyous" might mean. He responded that we ask God to "protect the people who are partying so they can party in peace, and not be disturbed by some mean dude." I think this is a brilliant interpretation. This prayer is no less than a plea for God to preserve celebration—that those who party may party in peace.

> So Christians unapologetically embrace that good, earthy gifts bring joy, even as we also proclaim an enduring joy that remains even when all pleasures are burned away.

We are called to party. But to practice celebration we need God's protection from despair, desolation, evil, and yes, from time to time, "mean dudes." Celebration itself is eternal, and in the here-and-now it is vital, and also fragile.

But we can embrace joy in a dark world, not as a saccharine act of denial or delusion, but because we know that delight flows from an unchanging source. True joy flows not from privilege or prosperity, but from the deepest springs of grace.

✦ ✦ ✦

Joy is both a gift and a practice, but it isn't primarily a feeling any more than self-control or faithfulness are feelings. It is a muscle we can strengthen with exercise.

Henri Nouwen described joy as "the experience of knowing that you are unconditionally loved and that nothing—sickness, failure, emotional distress, oppression, war, or even death—can take that love away." He explains that joy doesn't happen to us by accident. We choose joy (or not) every day. "It is a choice," he says, "based on the knowledge that we belong to God and have found in God our refuge and our safety and that nothing . . . can take God away from us."

Because joy comes from "the knowledge of God's love for us," it remains even when we meet disappointment or grief. Nouwen writes, "We are inclined to think that when we are sad, we cannot be glad, but in the life of a God-centered person, sorrow and joy can exist together."[3]

To practice joy is not to cultivate optimism, affect cheerfulness, or downplay pain. Like a swimmer practices strokes or a yogi does downward dogs, we intentionally and habitually open ourselves to God's unconditional love. We practice living in the reality that his love is deeper and more substantial than any need we could present to God.

The band Modest Mouse has a great album with an equally great title: Good News for People Who Love Bad News. There are Christians who paper over doubt and discouragement, painting spirituality as happy-clappy exuberance with no room for lament or sadness. But there are also those of us who love bad news. We can revel in the darkness and, however unintentionally, ignore the light in the name of gritty authenticity. We nurse each doubt, count each regret, and guard against pain by dismissing hope. We have to learn, through practice, to be people who embrace good news (even for people who love bad news).

Joy in the midst of darkness should never be faked or performed, but it can be chosen. And it is a vulnerable and courageous choice.

To choose joy is to see all existence as a gift, which is why the practice of joy is inseparable from the practice of gratitude. Gratitude gives birth to joy because gratitude teaches us to receive life as a gift in the moment we're in, regardless of what lies ahead. "It is the truly converted life in which God has become the center of all," Nouwen says. "There, gratitude is joy and joy is gratitude and everything becomes a surprising sign of God's presence."[4]

> To choose joy is to see all existence as a gift, which is why the practice of joy is inseparable from the practice of gratitude.

✦ ✦ ✦

During the uncertainty of my new pregnancy, a spiritual director at my church recommended that I pray a "prayer of indifference." Practicing this type of prayer is an act of releasing our grip on our own control, plans, even desires, and abandoning ourselves to the wild will of God, wherever that may lead.

Millennia ago, another new mother prayed a prayer of indifference. When Mary met an angel who told her that she would birth a son, she did not immediately jump for joy. She was "greatly troubled." Young and likely scared, Mary was tossed into the deep end of a mystery. She wasn't naive. She knew that joy doesn't come cheaply. She knew that joy must be shielded. She was troubled, and though her trouble was likely more extreme than the rest of us (not many of us have seen an angel), anyone who has waited, suspended between joy and pain, knows something of the mix of awe and terror, hope and fear, that Mary knew that day. But in her response to the angel, we see her pivot to a place of joy: "I am the servant of the Lord; let it be to me according to your word" (Luke 1:38). In this moment we see a pattern of prayer. Mary trusts God. She says, whether with enthusiasm or with a sigh, "Okay, I'm your servant. Do what you will."

This is the prayer the spiritual director challenged me to pray.

And I told her no. I protested. I told her that after a difficult few years and two miscarriages, it wasn't hard for me to believe that this pregnancy too might end in tragedy; what felt like a stretch was to let myself hope, to allow myself to desire something honestly before God. I didn't want to be indifferent! I wanted to open myself up to the risk of yearning, of celebration, even if that meant more disappointment down the road. We aren't Buddhists, I objected; we don't have to deny the goodness of desire. Christian faith does not see desire itself as bad or as the root of suffering. The call to indifference sounded to me like a call to neutrality, to denying what I wanted in exchange for a prim piety. So I argued.

She responded patiently. The prayer of indifference, she said, doesn't deny what we desire. It does not ask us to be dishonest before God. Instead, in this form of prayer we allow ourselves to admit our desires to God and to ourselves but to trust God enough to let him relativize our own longing. A prayer of indifference does not deny the goodness of desire, but it is a decision—as far as we are able—to desire God more. With this prayer, we ask to want whatever God wants. Mary's response is a pattern we take up. This strange way of prayer—and of life—births joy: "Let it be to me according to your word."

I will admit that, to me, this kind of prayer still seems like the stuff of spiritual black belts. To hold desire and trust, longing and holy indifference, together seems like an unattainable level of spiritual mastery. But I have a prayer to pray and a pattern to follow.

Flannery O'Connor's humility about her own desire and suffering gives me hope. When she was sick, only in her thirties and dying of lupus, she wrote to a friend: "I can, with one eye squinted, take it all as a blessing."[5] This is the kind of abandonment that leads to joy. God is trustworthy and what he gives is a blessing, even if we have to squint to see it.

> *To hold desire and trust, longing and holy indifference, together seems like an unattainable level of spiritual mastery.*

✦ ✦ ✦

Love and loss are a double helix this side of heaven. You can't have one without the other. God's calling on our lives will inevitably require us to risk both. We know this dappled reality in the most meaningful parts of our life: in struggling through marriage or singleness and celibacy, in loving and raising children, in our work, in serving the church.

Whenever I pray "shield the joyous," I think of my youngest daughter. Her brown eyes are the brightest I've ever seen. She is buoyant and luminous and seems to have come out of the womb laughing. Every maternal impulse in me is to keep her jubilant innocence alive. I do not want her eyes dimmed by grief. I do not want her to know the hardness of life. And yet my prayer that she'd be kept from all pain is often rooted in fear and distrust, not faith.

If Mary's son, the giver of all joy, knew anguish, my daughter will as well. So when I pray that God would "shield the joyous," I am not praying that God will make all circumstances work in her favor or that her joy will never be mingled with grief.

Instead, we pray that God himself would shield us, that as lesser delights dissolve in the face of pain, we might slowly find where enduring joy lies. And we pray that far under the surface of our lives, however easy or arduous, there would be a deep source of joy, a constant current of love that will never run dry.

Part Four

Culmination

This is the message we have heard from him and proclaim to you, that God is light, and in him is no darkness at all.

1 JOHN 1:5

*In this scene set in shadows
Like the night is here to stay,
There is evil cast around us
But it's love that wrote the play.*

DAVID WILCOX, "SHOW THE WAY"

13

And All for Your Love's Sake

Dawn

THE CHRISTIAN LIFE is more like a poem than an encyclopedia.

The poet Scott Cairns writes, "One of the reasons I enjoy poetry . . . is that a good poem insists that a reader learn to honor ambiguity, that he learn to collaborate with a poem's suggestive possibilities. . . . That is to say, a great poem—even a pretty good one—isn't ever done saying what it has to say."[1] What's true of poetry is true of the Christian life as well. Perplexity is built into the Christian faith. It is by nature perplexing. Ours is not primarily a faith of explanation, but of salvation.

This is not to say that Christianity is entirely an enigma, or a wax nose we shape to our liking. The Christian life is not an encyclopedia, but neither is it free verse. Like poetry, it has restraints—even rules, like a sonnet. Christian doctrine is our grammar and syntax; it provides the coherence of the Christian life. To reject doctrinal truth for a self-made, free-form faith makes as much sense as a poet rejecting the alphabet or words themselves. These truths from Scripture, handed to us through the church, are the only way into the poem itself. If we abandon them, we'll miss the poetry. And yet, like a poem, letters or words aren't the end in themselves, but tools that pull us into something greater. The end is not the alphabet or the structure of the sonnet, but the mystery and meaning revealed therein, which in Christianity is the triune God himself. Yet, in the poetry of the Christian life—its creeds, worship, and ethics—there is always a remainder, a space that we cannot pin down neatly. There is much we cannot know of God.

Therefore, to be a Christian is to honor ambiguity. It requires a willingness to endure mystery and to admit that there are limits to human knowledge. God has us on a "need to know basis," and there is much it seems that we don't need to know.

But if we are to trust God at all in the midst of such perplexity, we must learn (and continue learning again and again) that if the Christian life is a poem, it is a love poem. That's not all there is to it. The poem also encompasses lament, anger, even wrath. It tells stories and makes lists. But the beating heart of the poem—and the key to understanding it, even a little—is a living, dying, and resurrecting God of love.

God is vaster and more mysterious than we can fathom, and yet he has revealed himself. He showed up and told us who he is. God has spoken. And what he has said, in Christ, is that he loves us and is for us. This is the fundamental poetry that orders all of our lives.

One of my favorite songs is by folk artist Julie Miller. It's called "The Speed of Light."[2] The song is on an album Miller wrote in a time of darkness. She was debilitated by fibromyalgia, and grieving the sudden death of her beloved brother.[3] In this season, she penned these words: "The only thing that doesn't change, makes everything else rearrange, is the speed of light, the speed of light. Your love for me must be the speed of light."

The speed of light in a vacuum—299,792,458 meters per second, more commonly denoted simply as c—is a universal physical constant. It is a fixed reality of the physical universe. In his soaring discussion of the theology and science of light, theologian Stratford Caldecott explains how, through the complexity of electromagnetic fields, light itself suffuses everything, holding together everything in existence. He quotes Oxford physicist Andrew Steane, who writes that "if it were not for this dance of energy and light, I would fall through the surface of the road into the interior of planet Earth—or to be more thorough and accurate, my body would dissipate entirely into a vapor of dust, and so would Earth."[4]

This world is full of beauty and horror, but the unchanging reality underneath it all is the love of God that creates, sustains, and redeems all things. It is the constant holding us together. It is closer to us than our very breath, and moves toward us faster than 299,792,458 meters per second. All our doubts, wanderings, fears, and joys revolve around the fixed point of God's love.

✦ ✦ ✦

If this Compline prayer walks us slowly through a long, dark night, this last line—"and all for your love's sake. Amen"—is the glint of sun rising in the East. The unshakable reality of love breaks across the shadows of vulnerability and death, and we see that this prayer can only be prayed if there is a God who loves us. We weep because we can lament to one who cares about our sorrow. We watch because we believe that Love will not abandon us. We work because God is restoring the world in love. We can sleep because God governs the cosmos out of love. Every sickness can be transformed by love. When we're weary, we are given rest because we are loved. Love meets us even in death, bearing blessing. In our suffering, we are comforted by Love. In affliction, God dwells with us in love. And every joy in life flows freely from the deep source of God's love. Everything we have asked of God—his tending, giving, blessing, soothing, pitying, shielding—is for the sake of his love.

This nighttime prayer—and indeed all prayers—are tribu-
taries that find their end in the roaring ocean of God's triune
love. So as we sit, tired, at the end of an
ordinary day, and pray Compline, the
most defining truth about us is that we
are beloved.

> *This nighttime prayer—and indeed all prayers—are tributaries that find their end in the roaring ocean of God's triune love.*

There is really no wrong way to pray.
You cannot fail at prayer, except by
giving it up altogether. But prayer can
malform us if we suspect we are praying
to a God who can barely stand us, who
is malevolent and angry and out to get
us, who rolls his eyes when we call to
him, who we have to convince to hear us. We don't pray to
check off a spiritual to do list, to be good girls and boys so that
God might throw us a bone, to put a quarter in an inert ma-
chine hoping it springs to life, or to coax an angry deity to take
it easy on us. We don't pray to convince God to see our needs.
He asks us to pray, to tell him what we most long for, because
he loves us deeply and devastatingly.

We enter the long craft of faith and the practice of prayer in
response to the steady fact that we are already loved. God's love
and devotion to us, not ours to him, is the source of prayer. He
is the first mover in prayer, the one who has been calling to us
before we could ever call to him. And he will not stop calling,
no matter how dark the night becomes. Light, not darkness, is
the constant.

Prayer itself is therefore a willingness to enter into ambiguity
and vulnerability, but it is the ambiguity and vulnerability of
finding ourselves loved and having to learn, again and again,
how to receive that love and to trust it to remain true.

For some of us, it's hard to believe we are loved because we
think (or have been told) that we are unlovable.

Others have heard that God loves us so many times that it's grown stale. It's old news. Our grandmother loves us too. It's nice. But it's certainly not the orienting fact of our life. It's not what's holding us together on our worst day.

One reason we pray is so that the love of God might cease to be a spent and musty idea and instead become our light—the illumination by which we see everything.

Taking up this Compline prayer, with its litany of human vulnerability, I recall that all the categories of suffering on earth are real and horrifying. But I also remember that they cannot separate us from the love of God. All of human life, our suffering and joy, our ordinary heartbreak and laughter, every moment of our lives, has meaning because our end is to discover ourselves to be in Christ, eternally beloved of God.

Our lives hold heartbreak, pain, doubt, and despair, and yet what remains, and always will remain, is the love of the one "whose beauty is past change," as Gerard Manley Hopkins wrote.[5] The anchor of all theodicy, and all Christian prayer and practice, is God's kindhearted love.

In the end, the only way to endure this mystery is to put the whole weight of our life on the love of God. And the only thing that makes enduring the mystery worth it, is if God does truly love us.

When my eldest daughter was very little, she would get stuck on certain questions. She'd ask the same thing for weeks, sometimes months, over and over again. Her dad and I would try to answer her as patiently as we could, for the eleventy billionth time.

There are two questions she asked over and over. The first has become a bit of family joke because now as a big kid, she doesn't remember how often she used to ask it. The latter is so tender that I don't joke about it because I identify with it so deeply.

First, around age two or three, for months, she'd ask, "What's your first name?" Her dad would answer, "Jonathan." "What's your middle name?" "Edward." "Headward?" she'd reply as if this was new and interesting information that he had not already told her three times that morning. "No, not 'headward,' Edward," he'd remind her. Then she'd continue, "What's your last name?" She'd ask all of us—me, Jonathan, strangers, anyone who was willing to tell her their full name. And she'd ask as many times as possible. Eventually, thank God, she stopped with that question.

Years later, a different question bubbled up: "Mama, do you love me?" "Daddy, do you love me?" She was a little older now and knew that she was asking the question a lot. She admitted so—she'd say, "I'm sorry I'm asking again." But she needed to hear the answer again and again. She didn't ask because we hadn't told her that we loved her, but because it's so easy to doubt it, to question whether it's true, to forget, to wonder whether the answer can be trusted. We all need to hear it over and over again.

I come to God, again and again, with all kinds of questions. But all of them, in one way or another, boil down to the two questions my daughter has asked me thousands of times: What is your name? Do you love me?

In the Scriptures, a person's name is always linked to their character—who they are and what they are like. My constant question to God is, What are you like? Can you be trusted? Are you good?

And I ask, do you love me? Will you tell me again? It's hard for me to remember and to believe. Are you a God of love? And is that love for me? Even here? Even now?

One night, not long after 2017 drew to a close, I had a dark and vivid dream. In it, I had a best friend. She was a lovely person in almost every way, and we were inseparable. But midway through the dream I found out she was a hired assassin.

She was generally kind and generous, but occasionally killed some people for work. In the dream, I was reeling not knowing how I could trust my longtime friend. Then I saw her list of targets, and I was next on the list.

She was honest with me about it. She didn't want to kill me, but this was her job. She had a decision to make. I pleaded with her to spare my life, to find another line of work. Then I woke up, bolt upright in a dark room.

In the silence of the night I knew the dream was about how I see God. I loved him; I had called him a friend for a long time, but I didn't trust him. He could be so lovely, but he also kept a hitlist. And I was on it.

This image of God as a hitman shows my own faithlessness, how very little I know of God.

God is not like a hitman who, despite appearances, harbors hidden malice. If God is out to get us in any way, it is not to destroy us, but to love us.

C. S. Lewis says that the chief danger most of us face is not to stop believing in God, but to come to believe "dreadful things about him."[6] The dread we feel is that we will discover, "So this is what God is really like." He can't be trusted.

The reason God is trustworthy is because God is love. And his love is not like ours. Our love—from the best to the worst of us—is more akin to day and night. It comes and goes, rises and falls. At times we love purely and nobly, and it is glorious. But it always fades and falters. The sun sets.

God's love is a constant, not night and day, but the speed of light. His love is the center of all things and there is no darkness in it. The love of God—not sickness or weariness or death or suffering or affliction or joy—is the fixed center of our lives and of eternity.

> God's love is a constant, not night and day, but the speed of light.

✦ ✦ ✦

There's an aphorism repeated often in the writings of the me-
dieval church: *per crucem ad lucem,* through the cross to the light.

God loves us passionately and wants to bring us joy and flourishing, but this doesn't preclude a cross. God's love is refracted
through the cross, which often makes it hard to see or recognize.
But if we are to learn to trust—to place the weight of our lives
on the love of God—we can only learn this through the cross.

We come to know and trust God's love more deeply through
our own crosses, the things that make us feel we cannot go on,
the things that make us tired—the job loss, the break up, the
sickness, the loneliness, the long struggle with sin, the es-
trangement from a friend, the disappointment, the deaths of
those we love, our own death.

I wish there were some easier way, some way to learn to trust
God that was paved with luxury and endless ease, but *per crucem
ad lucem:* the way to the light runs smack dab through darkness—
or more accurately, we discover the light speeding toward us in
these very dark places.

And certainly the reality of the changeless love of God
doesn't mean we always *feel* God's love or God's nearness. Often
in seasons of suffering it feels like God is nowhere to be found.

God's love does not extinguish sorrow. Not yet, anyway. His
love is steadfast but incalculable, gentle but untamable. It is not
bound by our opinions. It shakes us yet sets us free. It slays us and
also teaches us how to live. It is as troubling as it is comforting. It
takes us as we are but insists on making us whole and vibrantly
alive—and that process is long and painful. God's raging and
unbounded love gives worth and purpose to all our vulnerability,
but it'll still hurt like hell to get through the day sometimes.

Instead of rescuing us from our vulnerability, God often calls
us more deeply into it. So to believe we are profoundly loved
means knowing that the disappointment and pain we encounter
is not because we are being rejected or ignored by God. "If we
ask . . . Why does God allow evil and suffering to continue?,"

writes Tim Keller, "and we look at the cross of Jesus, we still do not know what the answer is. However, we know what the answer isn't. It can't be that he doesn't love us."[7]

In the end, *per crucum ad lucem*, this pilgrimage to the light, does not run only through our own crosses, but through the cross of Jesus.

Jesus said, "Greater love has no one than this, that someone lay down his life for his friends" (John 15:13). And he did. Unlike the friend in my dream who arbitrarily took lives, he laid down his own life for us. The darkness of death was broken by his luminescent love.

When we see the love of Jesus, we see the fullness of God. Here is what I am slowly stretching to believe: there is no shadow side of God; no hidden deception or darkness behind the God revealed in Jesus. The God we pray to is the God who loves us—endlessly, relentlessly, patiently, and powerfully.

The culmination of this prayer and the culmination of all of history—including our own lives—is "and all for your love's sake. Amen." The love of God has the last word.

The Scriptures tell us that "for those who love God all things work together for good, for those who are called according to his purpose" (Romans 8:28). Like a resourceful farmhand, God puts everything to use. It's all raw material in his redemptive work.

But although God uses everything, he does not *cause* suffering as a means to some greater good. God himself is the greatest good, and he judges—and ultimately defeats and destroys—anything that does not flow from his goodness.

> *In the end darkness is not explained; it is defeated.*

In the end, darkness is not explained; it is defeated. Night is not justified or solved; it is endured until light overcomes it and it is no more.

In the meantime, we do not stop asking our questions of God. He allows us to ask them when we need to because he loves us. And we bring our perplexity into the prayers and practices of the church so that they can shape and direct our own questions.

Through its prayers, practices, and gathered worship, the church tells us over and over again, "This is what God is like. This is his name. This is how you know he loves you."

Together, we endure a mystery; we dwell in the already and not yet. But we do not only *endure* a mystery, we also *proclaim* a mystery. On Sunday, when I celebrate communion, I say to the congregation, "Let us proclaim the mystery of faith." And we say together,

Christ has died.
Christ is risen.
Christ will come again.

Christ entered entirely into our sadness, our sickness, our affliction, our weariness, our suffering, our death. Yet he lives, and will set all things to right.

In this same Eucharistic liturgy, we pray, "In the fullness of time, put all things in subjection under your Christ, and bring us with all your saints into the joy of your heavenly kingdom, where we shall see our Lord face to face."

In this meantime, we weep, watch, and work amid darkness and vulnerability. We are given the Scriptures, the church, the practices of our faith, and the gift of prayer. And I will continue to walk the path I've been given, through the cross to the light, and to ask these questions: "What are you like? Do you love us?" until we can ask them to our Lord face to face.

And in that instant, all of our clanging doubts and faithful questions will fade to silence. What we tasted for brief moments, what we longed for, and what we reached for, however feebly, in these ancient prayers and practices, we will know in full. For we have seen the light whom darkness could not overcome. We have met the unchangeable reality of love. And we will know that it was all for Love's sake.

Acknowledgments

THANK YOU TO CINDY BUNCH, Ethan McCarthy, and the whole team at IVP, who are not only talented and hardworking but also lovely human beings.

Endless thanks to Church of the Ascension in Pittsburgh, especially Jonathan and Andrea Millard and all Ascension staff and lay leadership. (And to Jim Wilson, for the chocolate.) You as a church have carried us through these years, and this book would not be possible without you.

Thanks to Hunter and Julie Dockery for being in my book and for showing me a God beautiful enough that he seemed worth trusting. Thanks also to Monica Lacy Bennett, Katy Hutson, Noel Jabbour, Amy Bornman, Jen Hemphill, and Steven and Bethany Hebbard for your friendship and for letting me share your ideas and stories in these pages. Thanks to Hannah and Andy Halfhill for being the accidental heroes of the preface, and being my friends even after I ruined your towels.

Thanks also to Alex and Jane Banfield-Hicks for letting me use their house to write and retreat, which allowed this book to be born. And to Ginger Stage, for asking and listening.

I am grateful for those readers, friends, Facebook friends, and Twitter followers who cheer on and share my work. They make it possible for me to do this.

There are too many deeply beloved friends to thank and I will never be able to list all of them, so I will not even make the attempt. But I want to thank my super-secret writing prayer team (though I cannot list all of you, I love and appreciate each of you and your prayers).

I could not do this without the help and encouragement of other writers. Thanks especially to Andy Crouch for being my writing career mentor (even though you never signed up for that). To Esau McCaulley, for all the phone calls. To Karen Swallow Prior and the Pelican Project squadron. To Wes Hill for your help thinking through this idea in its early stages. And to Andrea Palpant Dilley, who provided feedback on portions of this manuscript and encouragement throughout writing.

Deepest thanks to Marcia Bosscher, always my second reader, for her help with editing and for praying and cheering me on. Thank you for listening to me whine and encouraging me to keep writing.

To Marilyn and Charlie Chislaghi who became like family to us in the years this book was gestating and being birthed. Thank you also for providing a quiet place to write.

To Woody Giles, my dear friend, who provided helpful feedback on this manuscript (and everything else in my life).

Thank you to my Georgia family, especially Sandra and Jerry Dover. And to the Texas crew, especially Laura and James Mayes and David and Laci Harrison (and their families). Deepest gratitude to my mom, Loraine, who never failed to let me crawl in her bed when I was scared of the dark.

Every word of this book is in part a memorial to my dad and to the sons we lost. I cannot wait to be with you again in the morning.

Finally, to my girls, Raine and Flannery, who have sacrificed so I could write. I cannot thank you enough. And to Gus, who we welcomed to the world just as I finished this manuscript. Knowing each of you and watching you grow is my favorite part of being alive. I love you and delight in you, and I dedicated this book to you, hoping that it might help remind you when you're grownups that you are always deeply loved.

Greatest thanks to my husband, Jonathan. By God's grace, we walked through these dark years and fell in love again through them. You are not only a supportive partner but a profound theologian whose energy, suggestions, and ideas have shaped me and this project. Thank you for everything.

And glory be to the Word, from whom any goodness in our little words flows, and by whom they will be redeemed. Send out your light and your truth, let them lead us.

Discussion Questions and Suggested Practices

THESE DISCUSSION QUESTIONS AND PRACTICES can be done individually or in a group. If used individually, the questions can serve as journal prompts.

For groups, the text has been divided into five sessions for a six-week study. The idea would be to read and discuss this book over five weeks and then conclude with a meal and praying Compline together on the final week (or another office if you meet during the day). They can be adapted for longer or shorter studies. You can also add open-ended questions like, "Which parts of this chapter most resonated with you? Why?"

The practices are designed to be an invitation rather than a checklist. Whether you are in a group or on your own, read through the practices for each session and try 1–3 each week. Then reflect on the experience with a group, with a friend, or in your journal.

SESSION 1

Discussion questions

PROLOGUE

1. Can you think of a time of emergency, anxiety, or vulnerability when a passage of Scripture, a song, a prayer, or a practice came to you? If you have a story like that, share it with your group or journal about it. How did it make you feel when you entered into those words or that practice?

2. The author says, "Faith, I've come to believe, is more craft than feeling. And prayer is our chief practice in the craft." What are the implications of faith being like a craft? How would that change how you approach worship and prayer?

CHAPTER 1

1. What is nighttime like for you? Is it a time of anxiety, peace, grief, distraction, or something else? How do you feel when you are in the dark?

2. Has there been a time in your life when prayer was difficult? Why?

3. Did you grow up around people who prayed? What was your "default" way of thinking about prayer growing up? Did you pray "other people's prayers"?

4. What are the advantages or disadvantages of praying "other people's prayers"?

CHAPTER 2

1. The author says, "In the most vulnerable and human moments of our lives, doctrine is unavoidable. When all else gives way, all of us, from atheists to monks, fall back on what we believe about the world, about ourselves, and about God." Was there a time of crisis or suffering when you fell back on doctrine or what you believe? Describe that experience, and say what underlying story or conviction carried you.

2. Is there a particular place in your life where you are keeping God on trial? Where your verdict on his goodness is contingent on a particular outcome?

3. The author highlights doctrine, but then says we can't hold the Christian story in our head as a mere fact. How do doctrine and practice go together when we are suffering or encountering vulnerability?

Practices

1. Sit alone and quietly in the night with no screens or work. Turn off the overhead lighting and use only lamps or candlelight. Reflect on what thoughts, feelings, or questions surface in this time.

2. Go without electric light completely for one night. Journal your thoughts about that experience.

3. Try different ways of prayer: compline or another scripted prayer, extemporaneous prayer, journaling. Pick a style of prayer that you don't normally do. You can find a version of Compline at tishharrisonwarren.com/prayer-in-the-night.

4. Journal about what "cairns" in your life have been most important to you. What practices have been given to you that keep you from getting lost?

5. Read the Gospel of Mark all the way through in one sitting, or over the course of a week. Highlight every way you see Jesus experiencing vulnerability and entering into our human experience.

SESSION 2

Discussion questions

CHAPTER 3

1. How do you grieve normal or ordinary suffering in your own life? Are there particular practices that have been helpful for you in doing so?

2. What do you do when you feel sorrow or sadness? Are there patterns or habits of distraction or anger that mask sorrow in your life? Where do you think you've learned these strategies for avoiding grief?

3. The author quotes Lauren Winner, who says, "What churches do less well is grieve. We lack a ritual for the long and tiring

process that is sorrow and loss." Is this true in your experience of the church? Have you ever seen the church grieve well or beautifully?

4. Is night a time when you find grief bubbling up or getting louder? Why or why not?

CHAPTER 4

1. How does eschatological hope, that all shall be well, change how we watch and wait in the present? How does the hope of the resurrection inform the particular struggles in your life right now?

2. Can you think of a time when you kept watch at night? What was that like? What did this experience teach you about waiting and watching as a metaphor for the whole Christian life?

3. How do you "stay awake" to God? What sorts of experiences wake you up to God's presence or activity in your life?

CHAPTER 5

1. Do you ever work at night? What is that like for you?

2. How does your daily work participate in the work of God's restoration of the world in both big and small ways?

3. Where do you see the assumption of "competitive agency" in the church, the world, or your own experience? Do you see ways in which we pit "thoughts and prayers" and action against one another?

Practices

1. Set aside time for grief. This could be one hour or one day, but let yourself feel uncomfortable feelings and sorrow. Pray, journal, cry, sit in silence, and allow time for grief.

2. Pray lament psalms out loud for a week. Here are some to try: Psalm 22, Psalm 44, Psalm 88. Memorize one of these psalms, or a portion of one of them, and recite it out loud from memory several times in one day.

3. Write a psalm of lament about your own life or about your work. Read several lament psalms first and use them as a template.

4. Journal or brainstorm with a friend ways that you see God at work in your life, in the church, or in your community. Make a list.

5. Go to an art museum or a beautiful place in nature. Think and journal about how this beauty reflects the beauty of God. What must God be like if beauty reflects something of his character?

6. Donate money or volunteer with a ministry or non-profit that is bringing restoration to the world in some way.

7. Write a prayer or liturgy for your own work or vocation, like Noel did in chapter five. Use it for a week and reflect on what that was like.

SESSION 3

Discussion questions

CHAPTER 6

1. Have you ever encountered anything unexplained, or a spiritual being—an angel, a ghost, a demon? How is the supernatural regarded in your current circles? How was it regarded in your circles growing up?

2. The author says that prayer often precedes belief. Was there a time that prayer or another spiritual practice preceded belief for you or for your children?

3. What are your sleep habits like? Have you ever figured out a problem you were struggling with or had a concept become clear after you slept?

CHAPTER 7

1. Recall a time when you were really sick. How did your perspective about what is important or necessary change through that experience?

2. How do you experience the reality of vulnerability in your body? Has that affected your spiritual life or your spiritual practices?

3. Does weakness in your body ever act as a *memento mori* for you? Does it remind you of your death or your limitations?

CHAPTER 8

1. Where have you seen "curated weakness" on display in our culture, in the church, or in your own life? How does this differ from true vulnerability?

2. How have you found rest when you have been weary? What practices or experiences have brought renewal?

CHAPTER 9

1. Have you ever prayed for healing for someone who nevertheless died or who remains sick? How did that experience affect your prayer life?

2. Are there ways you have observed sentimentality or resistance to death in the church? The author quotes David Bentley Hart, who says, "Our faith is in a God who has come to rescue his creation from the absurdity of sin, the emptiness and waste of death, the forces—whether calculating malevolence or imbecile chance—that shatter living souls; and so we are permitted to hate these things with a perfect hatred." How does it change our spiritual life that we are permitted to hate death and suffering with the hatred that God feels for these enemies?

3. How have you experienced blessing in your own life? How do you reconcile blessing with suffering and death in your own experience?

Practices

1. Work on your sleep hygiene. Create a routine for bedtime that includes a consistent bedtime, comfort activities, and asking God to protect you with his angels, and follow it for a week (or more).

2. Write a letter to your body. Thank your body for the ways in which it has given you life and joy. Express frustration for the ways you have experienced the fall and limitations in your body. Describe what you've learned from your embodiment.

3. Practice silent prayer. Turn off your phone and put away any distractions. Sit in God's presence. As thoughts occur to you, acknowledge them and then let them go. Keep returning again to mental and verbal stillness before God. If this is the first time you've tried this, set a timer for five minutes. It can sometimes help to light a candle and to keep your eyes focused on it during the time of silence.

4. Read the story of Lazarus in John 11. Meditate on Jesus' "great distress" when he stands before the tomb. What do you think his face looked like? What did his body posture look like? How was he interacting with those around him?

5. Take up the Benedictine practice of remembering your death. Here are a few ways to do that: (A) Attend an Ash Wednesday service. (B) Journal about what you would want people to say about you at your eulogy, and what you would need to do now to become that person. (C) Journal about how physical limitations—sickness, sleep, grief—remind you of death and cause you to experience death in doses over the course of your life.

SESSION 4

Discussion questions

CHAPTER 10

1. The author discusses how moonflowers grow only at night. Are there particular parts of the spiritual life that "grow only at night"? What have you found growing in your own life during times of struggle or hardship?

2. The author describes the difference between the "theology of glory" and the "theology of the cross." Are there areas in your life where you have an implicit theology of glory? How about in our culture more generally?

3. In what ways have you known God as a comforter? How is that comfort similar to or different from what you naturally expect or think about comfort?

4. Do you agree that as a culture we rush to get over grief? Do you rush through your own suffering? Where do you see signs of this in your own life or in the surrounding culture?

CHAPTER 11

1. The author writes, "We often don't know how to walk with people when the road is long and there will likely be no happy ending." How have you seen the church care for the afflicted well or fail to do so? How might your own church or community care well for people with chronic and long-term pain or need?

2. The author quotes her friend Steven saying that he wants people to "seek Jesus where he promises to be found," and she adds that it is often among the poor, the needy, and the afflicted. How have you encountered Jesus in your own affliction or among the afflicted? Can you share what that experience has been like for you?

3. The author discusses how the gospel itself brings affliction to us. Have you seen this firsthand in your own life or someone close to you? How do you or the person you love trust God or struggle with trust in the midst of affliction?

4. The author writes, "Often the most foundational and shaping spiritual practices of our lives are things we'd never have chosen." Have you found a kind of spiritual formation in parts of your life that were unchosen? How have these unchosen things shaped and formed you, your community, or your view of God?

Practices

1. Choose an ascetic practice of some sort. This should be a practice that gives up some kind of comfort or pleasure. You could try fasting, partial fasting (giving up just one item, like meat), getting up extra early, or something else. Try this for a day, a few days, or a week. Journal about or share with your group anything you notice about this time. Are you more attuned to spiritual things? Are you more grumpy or short-tempered, more tired or hungry, more sad or anxious?

2. Take stock over a week or a month what things you go to habitually to cheer you up or soothe pain. Write these down and ask yourself what you enjoy, gain from, or get out of these things or experiences. Consider fasting from one for a time (even just for a day) and then coming back to it. How did time away from your creature comfort change how you think about it or interact with it?

3. Spend time with an individual, or volunteer to be with a community, that faces ongoing suffering or affliction. How do you encounter Jesus in this person or people?

4. Commit to praying for an extended season—a month, a quarter, or a year—for a particular community that experiences affliction. Pray that God would pity them, and ask God how he would have you aid the afflicted.

SESSION 5

Discussion questions

CHAPTER 12

1. Has joy ever felt "risky" to you? The author says that, out of self-protection, she often doesn't let herself feel joy. Does that resonate with you? Why or why not? How do you choose joy in spite of or even because of the risk associated with it?

2. The author says that Christians have a sacramental understanding of reality, which she explains means that "the stuff of earth carries within it the sacred presence of God." How does this view change how we experience creation and moments of beauty or pleasure?

3. The author says that joy is less a feeling than a muscle we need to exercise. What can you do this week to "put on" or "take up" joy as a commitment and an exercise?

4. The author mentions the Modest Mouse album *Good News for People Who Love Bad News*. Some people tend to be more melancholy and pessimistic, and others are naturally more optimistic. But pessimism and optimism can both be out of touch with reality, whereas joy is being connected to the hope that the deepest thing in reality is the love of God. To which way does your personality naturally gravitate? How can you grow toward the reality of the Christian hope?

CHAPTER 13

1. The author says that the Christian faith is true, but in a way that is more like a poem than an encyclopedia article in that there is ambiguity and perplexity built into our experience of faith. Do you read the Scriptures and see your life in Christ in this way? How does seeing the truth of Christianity in this way change things for you?

2. The author says that the love of God is like the speed of light. It's the one constant thing that makes everything else rearrange, and therefore it's the only thing that's worth staking a life on. What does it look like to stake your life on the love of God? Who do you know who has done this? What is distinctive about their life?

3. The author notes how the love of God can seem unreal either because we have been told that we are unlovable, or because it seems irrelevant to our daily lives. She discusses how prayer helps us place "the whole weight" of our life on God's love. What can you do this week (this month? this year?) to place more trust in the love of God?

4. The author says that all of our questions about God that emerge from a world of suffering and vulnerability come down to two questions: *What are you like? And can you be trusted?* How do the incarnation, death, and resurrection of Jesus help us to answer these questions about God? What helps you keep these truths foremost in your mind and heart when you are suffering, or just on an ordinary day?

5. Throughout the book, the author has talked about how practices hold together the reality of human vulnerability and the trustworthiness of God in a dynamic tension. Name Christian practices that you partake in and discuss how they hold these two realities in your own life.

Practices

1. The author describes how her daughter was "praying in pencil and crayon." Take a quiet moment of prayer and draw or paint something for which you are hoping or longing. Present that drawing before God as a way to reach for hope and then, as much as you are able, release it to God and pray over it a prayer of indifference: "Let it be to me according to your word."

2. Go on a "gratitude" walk. Walk or hike and spend the time intentionally noticing beauty, gifts, and any goodness in your life and thank God for it.

3. Practice celebration in a concrete way. Pick a liturgical feast day or milestone in your own or someone else's life (or just celebrate getting home from work on an average Wednesday!). Have a good meal, play your favorite music, and gather friends or family (this could be one other person or a group). Write a liturgy of celebration, where you pray a psalm (a few suggestions: Ps 112, Ps 136, Ps 145) and thank God for his gifts.

4. The author writes that we come to believe more in the love of God for us by placing the weight of our life and decisions on God's love. Think of one thing you would do if you absolutely believed God loved you, deeply and entirely. Take one small step of trust toward that thing this week.

   Read Romans 8 several times and meditate on one word or phrase from the chapter. Ask God what he would like you to do in response to that word or phrase. (If you are familiar with lectio divina, practice lectio divina with Romans 8). Journal about that time of meditation.

5. Go to church and, if you are a baptized Christian, take part in the Eucharist or Communion. Or, alternatively, witness a baptism (or be baptized yourself if you have not been). Take special notice of how death and love, darkness and light, are spoken of and dealt with in these sacraments.

Notes

PROLOGUE

[1]Following the pattern of Scripture, I use masculine pronouns to refer to God. I am aware that some readers will be uncomfortable with masculine language for God. I know that God is not male and that both male and female are equally made in the image of God. But given the limitations of the English language, the only options we have are a gendered pronoun (he or she) or avoiding pronouns altogether. Avoiding pronouns can make for a clinical, impersonal tone to sentences about God. I will therefore follow tradition and Scripture in using male pronouns, though I ask for grace from my readers who find this challenging.

[2]Richard Dawkins, *The God Delusion* (New York: Houghton Mifflin, 2008), 161.

[3]Madeleine L'Engle, *Walking on Water: Reflections on Faith and Art* (New York: North Point Press, 2001), 24.

[4]Tish Harrison Warren, "By the Book," *Comment*, December 1, 2016, www .cardus.ca/comment/article/by-the-book/.

1. FINDING COMPLINE

[1]The works of the left hand are also called the "alien works" of God. See the explanation in Veli-Matti Kärkkäinen, "'Evil, Love and the Left Hand of God': The Contribution of Luther's Theology of the Cross to an Evangelical Theology of Evil," *Evangelical Quarterly* 74, no. 3 (2002): 222-23.

[2]See, e.g., Edwin Eland, *The Layman's Guide to the Book of Common Prayer* (London: Longmans, Green & Co., 1896), 17.

[3]A. Roger Ekirch, *At Day's Close: Night in Times Past* (New York: W. W. Norton, 2005), 8.

[4]Edmund Burke, *A Philosophical Inquiry into the Origin of Our Ideas of the Sublime and the Beautiful*, in *The Works of Edmund Burke*, vol. 1 (London, 1846), iv.xiv, 155-56.

[5]William Shakespeare, *The Rape of Lucrece* (New York: Thomas Y. Crowell Co., 1912), 34.

[6]John of the Cross, *Dark Night of the Soul*, trans. Marabai Starr (New York: Riverhead Books, 2002).

[7]Quoted in Robert Taft, *Liturgy of the Hours East and West* (Collegeville, MN: The Liturgical Press, 1993), 18.

[8]Quoted in Taft, *Liturgy of the Hours*, 86. The version of the Bible that Basil cited numbered the psalms differently than our modern versions do, so his Psalm 90 is our Psalm 91.

[9]Both men and women express anxiety about the night, but women experience their vulnerability more acutely at night. See, e.g., Emily Badger, "This Is How Women Feel About Walking Alone at Night in Their Own Neighborhoods," *Washington Post*, May 28, 2014, www.washingtonpost.com/news/wonk /wp/2014/05/28/this-is-how-women-feel-about-walking-alone-at-night-in -their-own-neighborhoods; Katy Guest, "Imagine if Men Were Afraid to Walk Home Alone at Night," *The Guardian*, October 8, 2018, www.theguardian.com /commentisfree/2018/oct/08/women-men-curfew-danger-fear; Elise Godfryd, "'A Girl Walks Home at Night' and Our Culture of Fear," *Michigan Daily*, October 10, 2019, www.michigandaily.com/section/arts/%E2%80%9C-girl-walks -home-alone-night%E2%80%9D-and-our-culture-fear.

[10]Anne Brontë, *The Poems of Anne Brontë*, ed. Edward Chitham (New York: MacMillan, 1979), 110.

[11]National Public Radio, "It's Four O'Clock (In the Morning) Somewhere," *All Things Considered*, October 19, 2013. https://www.npr.org/templates/story/story .php?storyId=237813527.

[12]Brené Brown, an expert on vulnerability, defines vulnerability as "uncertainty, risk, and emotional exposure." See, e.g., Brené Brown, *Rising Strong: How the Ability to Reset Transforms the Way We Live, Love, Parent, and Lead* (New York: Random House, 2015), 274. The term has a range of meaning, and the way I'm using the word overlaps with Brown's framework. However, I am using the term in a slightly different way than she does, to highlight our capacity or susceptibility to be wounded and even destroyed in body, mind, and spirit. In this sense, being vulnerable is a fact of human existence before it is a chosen state.

[13]I recognize that, depending on one's geography, night does not always fall each twenty-four hours. In summer nearer to the arctic, you may not see true darkness for months, but then have long stretches of darkness in the winter. This also is a bodily experience of vulnerability.

[14]Kenneth Peterson, *Prayer as Night Falls* (Brewster, MA: Paraclete Press, 2013), chapters 1 and 2.

[15]Vicki Black, *Welcome to the Book of Common Prayer* (New York: Church Publishing, 2005), 63-64.

[16]Al Mohler, "Nearing the End—A Conversation with Theologian Stanley Hauerwas," *Thinking in Public*, April 28, 2014, https://albertmohler.com/2014/04/28 /nearing-the-end-a-conversation-with-theologian-stanley-hauerwas.

[17]Simon Chan, *Liturgical Theology* (Downers Grove, IL: IVP Academic, 2006), 48-52. Aidan Kavanaugh notes that the patristic maxim is actually *lex orandi statuat lex supplicandi*, and that "the predicate *statuat* does not permit these two fundamental laws of belief and worship in Christian life to float apart or to be opposed to each other, as in the 'tag' form *lex orandi, lex credendi*. The verb *statuat* articulates the standard of believing and the standard of worshiping within the faithful assembly." Aidan Kavanaugh, *On Liturgical Theology* (Collegeville, MN: Pueblo Publishing, 1984), 46.

[18]Marion Hatchett, *Commentary on the American Prayer Book* (New York: Harper Collins, 1995), 147.

[19]There is a whole genre of Christian literature on dealing with catastrophic loss. Often these books are written after the author has suffered life-altering tragedy, like the loss of a child or spouse. This book is about more ordinary forms of suffering. If you would like to read more about God's presence in the midst of catastrophic loss, I recommend Cameron Cole, *Therefore I Have Hope: 12 Truths that Comfort, Sustain, and Redeem in Tragedy* (Wheaton, IL: Crossway, 2018); Jerry Sittser, *A Grace Disguised: How the Soul Grows Through Loss* (Grand Rapids, MI: Zondervan, 2004); Nicholas Wolterstorff, *Lament for a Son* (Grand Rapids, MI: Eerdmans, 1987).

2. KEEP WATCH, DEAR LORD

[1]Over the Rhine, "Who Will Guard the Door?" *Drunkard's Prayer* (Back Porch Records, 2005).

[2]I owe this distinction to Tom Long's powerful, pastoral exploration of theodicy, Tom Long, *What Shall We Say? Evil, Suffering, and the Crisis of Faith* (Grand Rapids, MI: Eerdmans, 2013).

[3]Barna Group, "Atheism Doubles Among Generation Z," *Barna.com*, January 24, 2018, www.barna.com/research/atheism-doubles-among-generation-z.

[4]The theologian Jürgen Moltmann coined the term "protest atheism" to describe this kind of unbelief. Jürgen Moltmann, *The Crucified God*, trans. R. A. Wilson and John Bowden (Minneapolis, MN: Fortress Press, 1993), 221-27.

[5]Samuel Beckett, *Endgame* (New York: Grove Press, 1958), 55.

[6]Francis Spufford, *Unapologetic* (New York: HarperOne, 2013), 87.

[7]Spufford, *Unapologetic*, 88.

[8]Alan Jacobs, *Shaming the Devil* (Grand Rapids, MI: Eerdmans, 2004), 77-81.

[9]Alasdair MacIntyre, *After Virtue*, Third Edition (South Bend, IN: University of Notre Dame Press, 2013), 14-15.

[10]See Kenneth Surin, *Theology and the Problem of Evil* (Eugene, OR: Wipf & Stock, 2004), 162-63.

[11]Flannery O'Connor, *Mystery and Manners* (New York: Farrar, Straus, & Giroux, 1969), 209.

[12]Avery Cardinal Dulles, *Models of the Church* (New York: Crown Publishing, 2002), 10.

[13]Cornelius Plantinga Jr., *Not the Way It's Supposed to Be* (Grand Rapids, MI: Eerdmans, 1996), 29-30; N. T. Wright, *Paul and the Faithfulness of God* (Minneapolis, MN: Fortress Press, 2013), 761: "The resurrection itself demonstrated that the real enemy was not 'the gentiles,' not even the horrible spectre of the pagan empire. The real enemy was Death itself, the ultimate anti-creation

force, with Sin—the personified power of evil, doing duty apparently at some points for 'the satan' itself—as its henchman."

[14]See the discussion in Charles Matthewes, *Evil and the Augustinian Tradition* (Cambridge: Cambridge University Press, 2001), 60-75.

[15]N. T. Wright speaks of the resurrection as the salvation of God that is "the reversal or undoing or defeat of death." Wright, *The Resurrection of the Son of God* (Minneapolis, MN: Fortress Press, 2003), 201.

[16]C. S. Lewis, *Till We Have Faces* (New York: Harcourt, 1984), 308.

[17]Spufford, *Unapologetic*, 107.

[18]*Catechism of the Catholic Church*, no. 309, www.vatican.va/archive/ccc_css/archive/catechism/p1s2c1p4.htm.

[19]Merritt Tierce, "At Sea," *The Paris Review*, November 18, 2016, www.theparisreview.org/blog/2016/11/18/at-sea.

[20]Tierce, "At Sea."

[21]Spufford, *Unapologetic*, 105.

3. THOSE WHO WEEP

[1]Walker Percy writes, "The greatness of the South, like the greatness of the English squirearchy, had always a stronger Greek flavor than it ever had a Christian. Its nobility and graciousness was the nobility and graciousness of the Old Stoa." Walker Percy, "Stoicism in the South," in *Signposts in a Strange Land* (New York: Picador, 2000), 84.

[2]Quoted in Sidney Mead, *The Lively Experiment: The Shaping of Christianity in America* (New York: Harper & Row, 1963), 4.

[3]Peter Leithart describes Americans as "boundlessly optimistic." Peter Leithart, *Between Babel and Beast* (Eugene, OR: Cascade, 2009), 57. Damon Linker argues that our optimism "also tends to blind us to the ineradicably tragic dimensions of life." Damon Linker, "American Optimism is Becoming a Problem," *The Week*, April 27, 2020, https://theweek.com/articles/911058/american-optimism-becoming-problem.

[4]Henri Nouwen, *A Letter of Consolation* (New York: Harper & Row, 1989), 7.

[5]Lauren Winner, *Mudhouse Sabbath* (Brewster, MA: Paraclete Press, 2007), 27.

[6]Robert Louis Wilken, *The First Thousand Years* (New Haven, CT: Yale University Press, 2012), 107.

[7]Tish Harrison Warren, "By the Book," *Cardus*, December 1, 2016, www.cardus.ca/comment/article/by-the-book.

[8]John Calvin, *Writings on Pastoral Piety*, trans. Elsie Anne McKee (New York: Paulist Press, 2001), 56.

[9]D. C. Schindler, *Freedom from Reality: The Diabolical Character of Modern Liberty* (South Bend, IN: University of Notre Dame Press, 2017), 147.

[10]J. Todd Billings, *Rejoicing in Lament: Wrestling with Incurable Cancer and Life in Christ* (Grand Rapids, MI: Brazos, 2015), 38.

[11]See Paul Burns, *A Model for the Christian Life: Hilary of Poitiers' Commentary on the Psalms* (Washington, DC: Catholic University of America Press, 2012), 54-57.

[12]Athanasius, "The Letter of St. Athanasius to Marcellinus on the Interpretation of the Psalms," in *On the Incarnation*, ed. John Behr (Crestwood, NY: St. Vladimir's Seminary Press, 1977), 103.

[13]Billings, *Rejoicing in Lament*, 42.

[14]N. T. Wright says, "The point of lament, woven thus into the fabric of the biblical tradition, is not just that it's an outlet for our frustration, sorrow, loneliness and sheer inability to understand what is happening or why. The mystery of the biblical story is that *God also laments*." N. T. Wright, "Christianity Offers No Ideas About the Coronavirus. It's Not Supposed To," *Time*, March 29, 2020, https://time.com/5808495/coronavirus-christianity.

[15]N. T. Wright, *The Case for the Psalms: Why They Are Essential* (New York: HarperOne, 2013), 136.

[16]Robert Louis Wilken, *The Spirit of Early Christian Thought* (New Haven, CT: Yale University Press, 2008), 315-17; see also Dietrich Bonhoeffer, *Psalms: The Prayerbook of the Bible* (Minneapolis, MN: Augsburg Press, 1966), 37-38.

[17]Thomas Long, *Accompany Them with Singing: The Christian Funeral* (Louisville, KY: Westminster John Knox, 2009), 38-40.

[18]See the powerful discussion in Frederick Dale Brunner, *The Gospel of John* (Grand Rapids, MI: Eerdmans, 2012), 679-80.

4. THOSE WHO WATCH

[1]C. S. Lewis, *A Grief Observed* (New York: HarperOne, 1994), 3.

[2]I want to be clear that I am not advocating that anyone stay in an abusive marriage. There are biblical reasons for which divorce is permissible—adultery, abuse, and abandonment. If you think you may be in an abusive relationship, please go to the National Domestic Violence Hotline: www.thehotline.org/help.

[3]Julian of Norwich, *Revelations of Divine Love* (New York: Oxford, 2015), 31, 78.

[4]I'm using *birdwatcher* and *birder* here interchangeably, but they are not the same thing, which is the kind of distinction that those in the birding community are intense about.

[5]Jonathan Rosen, "The Difference Between Bird Watching and Birding, *New Yorker*, October 17, 2011, www.newyorker.com/books/page-turner/the-difference-between-bird-watching-and-birding.

[6]Bill Thompson III, "Top 10 Long-Awaited Signs of Spring," *Birdwatcher's Digest*, www.birdwatchersdigest.com/bwdsite/learn/top10/signs-of-spring.php.

[7]Rowan Williams, *Being Disciples* (Grand Rapids, MI: Eerdmans, 2016), 5.

[8]Nicholas Carr, *The Shallows: What the Internet Is Doing to Our Brains* (New York: WW Norton & Co, 2011), 90, 137.

[9] Oliver O'Donovan, *Self, World, and Time*, vol. 1, *Ethics as Theology: An Induction* (Grand Rapids, MI: Eerdmans, 2013), 8.

[10] Simone Weil, "Attention and Will," in *Simone Weil: An Anthology*, ed. Sian Miles (New York: Grove Books, 2000), 212.

5. THOSE WHO WORK

[1] A. Roger Ekirch notes that most people in the middle ages did not work after dark. In fact, nocturnal labor was forbidden in most trades. However, some people did work at night and this appears to be mostly the poor. But he notes that it was not until the early modern era that working at night began to grow more common. Additionally, even though people weren't working at night, they were not sleeping the whole time either. Ekirch describes the distinction discussed between "first sleep" and "second sleep" that begins to decline by the 17th century. The intervening period of wakefulness was sometimes called "the watch." Though this is interesting in light of the topics of this book, it isn't immediately relevant to us today, so I did not include a discussion of it. A. Roger Ekirch, *At Day's Close: Night in Times Past* (New York: W. W. Norton, 2005), 155-56, 300-305.

[2] Thanks to Kirk Botula for this insight. He made this point in a talk at Jubilee Professional a couple of years ago. He shows that there are many images of Adam and Eve before the fall and some of them working post-fall, but relatively few of them working before the fall.

[3] The literature on early Christian philanthropy is massive. Here are a few accessible introductions: Alvin Schmidt, *How Christianity Changed the World* (Grand Rapids, MI: Zondervan, 2009); Tom Holland, *Dominion* (New York: Basic Books, 2019); *Wealth and Poverty in Early Church and Society*, ed. Susan Holman (Grand Rapids, MI: Baker Academic, 2008); David Bentley Hart, *The Story of Christianity* (New York: Hachette, 2013); Timothy Miller, *The Birth of the Hospital in the Byzantine Empire* (Baltimore, MD: Johns Hopkins University Press, 1997).

[4] You can order your own copy of her book here: www.katyhutson.com/limited-edition-poetry-book/now-i-lay-me-down-to-fight-signed-first-edition.

[5] Tracy Jan, "They Said I Was Going to Work Like a Donkey. I Was Grateful," *Washington Post*, July 11, 2017, www.washingtonpost.com/news/wonk/wp/2017/07/11/they-said-i-was-going-to-work-like-a-donkey-i-was-grateful.

[6] Lesslie Newbigin, *Signs Amid the Rubble* (Grand Rapids, MI: Eerdmans, 2003), 47.

[7] Scholars debate the source of this idea, but there seems to be general agreement that it has its origins in the Renaissance humanism that generated what Louis Dupré called the "passage to modernity." Dupré, *Passage to Modernity* (New Haven, CT: Yale University Press, 1993), especially 113 and 125. See also Michael Allen Gillespie, *The Theological Origins of Modernity* (Chicago: University of Chicago Press, 2008), 32-35.

[8]Daniel Sloss, "Dark," Netflix, 2018.

[9]Justin Rosolino, *Idiot, Sojourning Soul: A Post-Secular Pilgrimage* (Eugene, OR: Resource Publications, 2020), 124.

[10]Steven Pinker, *Enlightenment Now: The Case for Reason, Science, Humanism, and Progress* (New York: Penguin, 2018), 63.

[11]Francis Spufford, *Unapologetic* (New York: HarperOne, 2013), 133.

[12]M. Eugene Boring, *Mark: A Commentary*, New Testament Library (Louisville, KY: Westminster John Knox, 2006), 164-65.

6. GIVE YOUR ANGELS CHARGE OVER THOSE WHO SLEEP

[1]Parts of this chapter have been adapted from Tish Harrison Warren, "Angels We Ignore on High," *Christianity Today*, December 20, 2013, www.christianity today.com/women/2013/december/angels-we-ignore-on-high.html.

[2]The disenchantment of the world and its literal emptying are related to each other, as a number of scholars have pointed out. Steven Vogel writes, "The project of enlightenment aims above all at the *domination of nature*. Disenchanted and objectified nature, appearing now in the guise of meaningless matter, is seen by enlightenment simply as something to be overcome and mastered for human purposes and not as something to be imitated, propitiated, or religiously celebrated. . . . The position of humans as themselves *part* of nature that mythic thought insists upon and mimesis acts out is thereby forgotten. The result is a fundamental separation of humans from nature." Steven Vogel, *Against Nature: The Concept of Nature in Critical Theory* (Albany: State University of New York Press, 1996), 52. Alister McGrath says that this disenchanted idea of nature is sometimes associated with Christianity, but that in reality it is foreign to the way the Scriptures and the Christian tradition describe nature. McGrath, *The Reenchantment of Nature: The Denial of Religion and the Ecological Crisis* (New York: Doubleday, 2002). See also Richard Bauckham, *The Bible and Ecology: Rediscovering the Community of Creation* (Waco, TX: Baylor University Press, 2010).

[3]Thomas Aquinas, *Summa Theologiae*, I, q 50, a 1, www.newadvent.org/summa /1050.htm.

[4]Pseudo-Dionysius, *The Celestial Hierarchy*, in *The Complete Works*, trans. Colm Luibhéid and Paul Rorem (New York: Paulist Press, 1987), 321A, 181.

[5]Hilary of Poitiers, quoted in Jean Danielou, *The Angels and Their Mission* (Manchester, NH: Sophia Institute Press, 2009), 90.

[6]Mike Cosper, *Recapturing the Wonder: Transcendent Faith in a Disenchanted World* (Downers Grove, IL: InterVarsity Press, 2017), 10.

[7]C. S. Lewis, *The Screwtape Letters and Screwtape Proposes a Toast* (New York: MacMillan, 1961), viii.

[8]Warren, "Angels We Ignore on High."

[9]Paul Kennedy, "On Radical Orthodoxy," Ideas Podcast, June 4, 2007, http://theologyphilosophycentre.co.uk/docs/mp3/ideas_20070604_2421.mp3.

[10]Cosper, *Recapturing the Wonder*, 142.

[11]Elizabeth Barrett Browning, *Aurora Leigh: A Poem* (Chicago: Academy Chicago Publishers, 1979), 265.

[12]Roxanne Stone, "James K. A. Smith: St. Augustine Might Just Be the Therapist We Need Today," *Religion News Service*, April 28, 2020, https://religionnews.com/2019/10/11/james-k-a-smith-st-augustine-might-just-be-the-therapist-we-need-today.

[13]See John Medina, *Brain Rules* (Seattle, WA: Pear Press, 2014), 41-51.

[14]James Bryan Smith, *The Good and Beautiful God: Falling in Love with the God Jesus Knows* (Downers Grove, IL: InterVarsity Press, 2009), 34.

[15]Cosper, *Recapturing the Wonder*, 118.

7. TEND THE SICK, LORD CHRIST

[1]Markham Heid, "Here's Why You Always Feel Sicker at Night," *Time*, February 6, 2019, https://time.com/5521313/why-you-feel-sicker-at-night/.

[2]David Wilcox, "Cold," *East Asheville Hardware* (1996).

[3]Jeremy Taylor, *Holy Living and Holy Dying Together with Prayers* (London, 1839), 396.

[4]Robert Half, "Are Your Co-Workers Making You Sick?" October 24, 2019, www.roberthalf.com/blog/management-tips/are-your-coworkers-making-you-sick.

[5]Beth Mirza, "Majority of Americans Report to Work When Sick," *SHRM Blog*, May 13, 2011, https://blog.shrm.org/workplace/majority-of-americans-report-to-work-when-sick.

[6]The Covid-19 pandemic exposed weaknesses in sick leave policies in America. See Allison Inserro, "COVID-19 Exposes Cracks in Paid Sick Leave Policies," AJMC, March 20, 2020, www.ajmc.com/view/covid19-exposes-cracks-in-paid-sick-leave-policies. Even many front-line workers were denied sick leave by employers. See Alexia Fernández Campbell, "McDonald's, Marriot Franchises Didn't Pay COVID-19 Sick Leave. That Was Illegal," The Center for Public Integrity, August 3, 2020, https://publicintegrity.org/inequality-poverty-opportunity/workers-rights/deny-paid-sick-leave-workers-coronavirus-pandemic-mcdonalds. It is not clear yet how—or if—the Covid-19 pandemic will impact the way we think about bodily limits, illness, or sick leave as a society.

[7]Scott Cairns, *The End of Suffering: Finding Purpose in Pain* (Brewster, MA: Paraclete Press, 2009), 21.

[8]Taylor, *Holy Living and Holy Dying*, 419.

[9]Cairns, *End of Suffering*, 21-22.

[10]The following is adapted from Tish Harrison Warren, "My Lord and Migraine," *The Well* (Blog), January 14, 2016, https://thewell.intervarsity.org/blog/my-lord-and-migraine.

8. GIVE REST TO THE WEARY

[1]Quoted in James Bryan Smith, *Rich Mullins: An Arrow Pointing to Heaven* (Nashville: B&H, 2002), 30.

[2]Cameron Crowe, director, *Almost Famous* (Culver City, CA: Columbia Pictures, 2000).

[3]Isaac the Syrian, *Mystic Treatises*, trans. A. J. Wensinck, viii, http://lesvoies.free .fr/spip/article.php?id_article=342.

[4]Craig Keener, *A Commentary on the Gospel of Matthew* (Grand Rapids, MI: Eerdmans, 1999), 348.

[5]Grant Osborne, *Matthew*, Exegetical Commentary on the New Testament (Grand Rapids, MI: Zondervan, 2010), 446.

[6]Doug Webster, *The Easy Yoke* (Colorado Springs, CO: NavPress, 1995), 8, 14.

[7]Quoted in Martin Laird, *Into the Silent Land* (New York: Oxford University Press, 2006), 27.

[8]Bradley Holt, *Thirsty for God: A Brief History of Christian Spirituality*, 3rd ed. (Minneapolis, MN: Fortress Press, 2017), 88-89.

[9]Holt, *Thirsty for God*, 88-89.

9. BLESS THE DYING

[1]An exception to this is the prosperity gospel, which was created on American soil and expresses a vanishingly small percentage of the global and historical church's view on suffering. See Ross Douthat, *Bad Religion: How We Became a Nation of Heretics* (New York: Free Press, 2012), 182-210.

[2]The service is available at http://justus.anglican.org/resources/bcp/1549/Visitation _Sick_1549.htm.

[3]David Bentley Hart, *The Doors of the Sea: Where Was God in the Tsunami?* (Grand Rapids, MI: Eerdmans, 2005), 101.

[4]N. T. Wright, "The Road to New Creation," NT Wright Page, September 23, 2006, http://ntwrightpage.com/2016/03/30/the-road-to-new-creation.

[5]Jonathan Pennington, *The Sermon on the Mount and Human Flourishing: A Theological Commentary* (Grand Rapids, MI: Baker Academic, 2017), 41-68.

[6]Pennington, *Sermon on the Mount*, 149.

[7]Jaroslav Pelikan, *The Shape of Death: Life, Death, and Immortality in the Early Fathers* (Nashville: Abingdon, 1961), 55.

[8]Benedict of Nursia, *The Rule of St. Benedict*, trans. Timothy Fry (New York: Vintage Books, 1998), 4.44-47, 13.

10. SOOTHE THE SUFFERING

[1]Simone Weil, *Gravity and Grace*, trans. Emma Crawford and Mario von der Ruhr (New York: Routledge, 2002), 81.

[2]Quoted in Scott Cairns, *The End of Suffering: Finding Purpose in Pain* (Brewster, MA: Paraclete Press, 2009), 11.

[3]Cairns, *The End of Suffering*, 11.

[4]Cairns, *The End of Suffering*, 11.

[5]Augustine, Sermon 341.12, *Sermons 341-400 on Various Themes*, trans. Edmund Hill, OP, The Works of St. Augustine for the 21st Century (Hyde Park, NY: New City Press, 1995), 27.

[6]Martin Luther, *Heidelberg Disputation* (1518), http://bookofconcord.org/heidel berg.php.

[7]C. FitzSimons Allison, *The Cruelty of Heresy* (New York: Morehouse Publishing, 1994), 31.

[8]Arcade Fire, "Creature Comfort," *Everything Now* (2017).

[9]Dennis Byrne, "We're a Nation of Addicts," *Chicago Tribune*, Feb 2, 2015, www .chicagotribune.com/opinion/commentary/ct-institute-of-drug-abuse-gallup -0203-20150202-story.html.

[10]Tommy Tomlinson, *The Elephant in the Room: One Fat Man's Quest to Get Smaller in a Growing America* (New York: Simon & Schuster, 2019), 100.

[11]Andrew Sullivan, "I Used to Be a Human Being," *New York Magazine*, September 19, 2016, http://nymag.com/intelligencer/2016/09/andrew-sullivan-my -distraction-sickness-and-yours.html.

[12]Pierre Teilhard de Chardin, *The Making of a Mind: Letters from a Soldier-Priest, 1914-1919* (New York: Harper & Row, 1961), 57-58.

[13]Friedrich Nietzsche, *Twilight of the Idols*, in *The Portable Nietzsche*, trans. Walter Kaufmann (New York: Penguin, 1976), 467.

[14]Marva Dawn, *Powers, Weakness, and the Tabernacling of God* (Grand Rapids, MI: Eerdmans, 2001), 47-48.

11. PITY THE AFFLICTED

[1]I don't recommend spending loads of time trying to parse out these categories with laser precision. This is prayer and poetry, not sociology. The point of the prayer is comfort either way.

[2]Jonathan Graff-Redford, "Sundowning: Late Day Confusion," *Mayo Clinic*, April 23, 2019, www.mayoclinic.org/diseases-conditions/alzheimers-disease /expert-answers/sundowning/faq-20058511.

[3]This is the same Steven, the "farmer-prophet," who makes an appearance in *Liturgy of the Ordinary*.

[4]A beautiful exploration of this idea is Kate Bowler's *Everything Happens for a Reason* (New York: Random House, 2018). One of the themes she explores is the way that the prosperity gospel subtly affects how we see God, whether we explicitly profess it or not.

[5]C. S. Lewis, "Answers to Questions on Christianity," in *God in the Dock* (Grand Rapids, MI: Eerdmans, 2014), 48.

[6]Aquinas, *Summa Theologiae*, II.II q 17 a 3, www.newadvent.org/summa/3017.htm.

[7]Ron Belgau, "Arduous Goods," *First Things*, August 22, 2013, www.firstthings .com/blogs/firstthoughts/2013/08/arduous-goods.

[8]Andy Crouch, *Strong and Weak* (Downers Grove, IL: InterVarsity Press, 2016), 31.

[9]Mother Teresa, *No Greater Love*, ed. Becky Benenate and Joseph Durepos (Novato, CA: New World Library, 1989), 166.

[10]Joseph Minich, *Enduring Divine Absence* (Leesburg, VA: Davenant Institute, 2018), 54.

[11]Quoted in Lacey Rose, "'He Just Knows What's Funny': Hollywood's Secret Comic Whisperer Finally Gets His Own Spotlight," *The Hollywood Reporter*, April 15, 2019, www.hollywoodreporter.com/features/chappelles-show-creator -neal-brennan-finally-gets-own-spotlight-1199871.

[12]Scott Sunquist, *The Unexpected Christian Century: The Reversal and Transformation of Global Christianity, 1900-2000* (Grand Rapids, MI: Baker Academic, 2015).

[13]Andrew Boyd, *Neither Bomb nor Bullet: Benjamin Kwashi: Archbishop on the Front Line* (Oxford: Lion Hudson, 2019), 9.

12. SHIELD THE JOYOUS

[1]C. S. Lewis wrote, "To love at all is to be vulnerable. Love anything, and your heart will certainly be wrung and possibly be broken. If you want to make sure of keeping it intact, you must give your heart to no one, not even to an animal. Wrap it carefully round with hobbies and little luxuries; avoid all entanglements; lock it up safe in the casket or coffin of your selfishness. But in that casket—safe, dark, motionless, airless—it will change. It will not be broken; it will become unbreakable, impenetrable, irredeemable. The alternative to tragedy, or at least to the risk of tragedy, is damnation. The only place outside Heaven where you can be perfectly safe from all the dangers and perturbations of love is Hell." C. S. Lewis, *The Four Loves* (New York: Harcourt. Brace & Co., 1960), 121.

[2]The literature here is vast, but good introductions to this idea can be found in Hans Boersma, *Heavenly Participation* (Grand Rapids, MI: Eerdmans, 2011); and Paul Tyson, *Returning to Reality* (Eugene, OR: Cascade, 2014).

[3]Henri Nouwen, *Here and Now: Living in the Spirit* (New York: Crossroad, 1994), 30-31.

[4]Nouwen, *Here and Now*, 26.

[5]Flannery O'Connor, *The Habit of Being*, ed. Sally Fitzgerald (New York: Farrar, Strauss, & Giroux, 1988), 57.

13. AND ALL FOR YOUR LOVE'S SAKE

[1]Scott Cairns, *The End of Suffering: Finding Purpose in Pain* (Brewster, MA: Paraclete Press, 2009), 101.

[2]Julie Miller, "Speed of Light," *Broken Things* (Hightone Records, 1999).

[3]Geoffrey Himes, "Buddy and Julie Miller Walk the Line," *Paste Magazine*, May 28, 2009, www.pastemagazine.com/articles/2009/05/buddy-julie-miller-walk -the-line.html.

[4]Stratford Caldecott, *The Radiance of Being: Dimensions of Cosmic Christianity* (Brooklyn, NY: Angelico Press, 2013), 12-14.

[5]Gerard Manley Hopkins, "Pied Beauty," www.poetryfoundation.org/poems /44399/pied-beauty.

[6]C. S. Lewis, *A Grief Observed* (New York: HarperCollins, 2001), 6.

[7]Tim Keller, *The Reason for God* (New York: Penguin, 2008), 31.

Also by
Tish Harrison Warren